What Difference Does Jesus Make?

What Difference Does Jesus Make?

F. J. Sheed

SHEED AND WARD • NEW YORK

Copyright © by Sheed and Ward, Inc., 1971

Library of Congress Catalog Card Number: 76-162382

Standard Book Number: 8362-1329-7 *(Library Edition)*
8362-1129-4 *(Paperback)*

Manufactured in the United States of America

To my Godchildren

who will react

variously

Contents

Introductory

More precisely, my title means "What needs have men here on earth today that only Christ Jesus can meet?" So we begin by looking at our world.

A hundred years ago, Matthew Arnold wrote of himself

> Wandering between two worlds, one dead,
> The other powerless to be born.

He might have been looking straight at us. Our world is not dead, but if I were its physician I should be alarmed about it. All its main structures and institutions—Family, State, Church—are showing great cracks. The standards and values by which it has lived are violently derided, and only pallidly defended. But there is no common idea of what the new world *ought* to be, or how it can be brought to be. Derision is not building stuff. We are in a time of crisis which could become chaos.

The Family is under the heaviest attack because each family, and each member of each family, is under daily pressure. Parental authority has become a sick joke, the uncertainty of parents as to what authority they have is equalled by the certainty of their children that they have none. Sexual morals are a shambles—not that everyone is living his sex life riotously, but that there are no standards left unchallenged—chastity and marital fidelity are as sick a joke as authority; abortion, lesbianism, sodomy, have quite suddenly become matters of personal taste.

In the larger sphere of Society and Government, the same processes are at work. Patriotism, respect for authority, are both corroded by the assumption that the lowest self-interest rules our rulers. Violence is the instant answer to every question, with young children taught to make their little bombs and place them where they can kill. In the sexual storm the majority still in a general way accept the old standards, just as in politics the majority are still patriotic, law-abiding, opposed to violence—but in both areas largely from habit. Their minds have not been active. They find the old standards good, but even to themselves they cannot state a convincing case for them: so they avoid talking to their children about them. The "silent majority," so often invoked, gives the effect of a quite singularly dumb majority. It will vote, but if things get beyond voting it does not seem likely to affect the issue.

The assailants of the old order, on the other hand, are articulate indeed: the whole sky rings with their voices. But there is not much actual thinking there. As we listen closely, we are driven to feel that all they have to offer is their derision, their scorn of all that is established. But scorn, while it may be a just criticism of the old order, provides no principles for a new. What it *can* do is make a country unmanageable.

That this is what it is in fact doing is shown by the phrase we hear everywhere, "Things can't go on like this"—a phrase as negative and unconstructive as scorn. What *can* things go on like? No more than the extremists of right and left have the mass of men any real answer to that. Individuals of all three sorts have their own conflicting prescriptions for a better world order. About none of them is there general agreement. Any one of them might be imposed by violence. If that happens, our world will indeed be dead.

General agreement is the missing element. For a human political order as distinct from a tyranny, a society must be agreed on how men should be treated, on what rights the individual has which the collective may not infringe. For this there must be agreement about man and about life. We are here. A while ago we were not. Not such a long while before that nobody was. In a while we shall not be. So what is it all about? Why are we here? What are we supposed to be doing? What comes after death? Does anything?

Without answers to these questions we cannot live life intelligently, we only play it by ear. And that is how our world is now playing it. No science even claims to give the answers. Unless religion can, they must stay unanswered.

But in this time of crisis which could become chaos, the Church is afflicted with the same problems as the world. With her children questioning her authority and even her relevance, she is preoccupied with her own renewal, tormented about her own restructuring. In what shape the Church may emerge I do not know. But Christ needs no renewal, defects in the Church's structure are not defects in him. His message needs no recasting, only deeper understanding of what it has in it for the world's needs. The lament he uttered over Jerusalem he might well be uttering over us—"If only you had known what things make for your peace" (Luke 19.42).

What he has to give the world trying to be born is the subject of this book.

Chapter I

The Dimming of Christ

Christ is in eclipse for many Christians in many Churches. I have felt it more graceful to choose examples from my own, but I fear that people of most Churches can translate them in terms of their own experience.

I

I was talking to several hundred first- and second-year boys and girls from the Catholic high schools of a town whose name is irrelevant. I put a question: "Apart from obeying the law of the Church, is there any point in going to Mass?"

We talked back and forth for forty minutes, but they could not think of any. They had all lived through eight years in the parochial schools and a year or so in high school, but not one of them could think of anything gained by going to Mass, or anything lost by staying away. And they were honestly trying. They and I were having a real conversation. They were a friendly group, obviously preferring me to whatever class I was keeping them from: even the boy who called what went on at the altar a lot of flummery bore no ill will to me personally. Some of the group had a devotion to the Mass, but they

3

were no more able than the rest to say what point there might be in it. Nobody mentioned Christ till I did. Nobody mentioned Communion either: they knew that you can receive it outside Mass, just as you can go to Mass without receiving it: yet I thought its non-mention odd. It was the Mass they were interested in—but from one angle only: why did they have to go on Sunday? There was not much profit in discussing that, I felt, till they saw some point in going at all. So to that I applied myself.

The Apostles' Creed says that Christ is in heaven sitting at the right hand of the Father, and I asked what he is *doing* there—sitting is not much of an occupation. The Epistle to the Hebrews says in chapter 9 that he entered heaven "on our behalf," which means that he is doing something there *for us*. What is it? From most there was no effort at an answer; what could it possibly matter? In some there was a feeling-out for the answer but no more. In no audience young or old has anyone ever quoted the phrase of the seventh chapter of that same Epistle: "He lives on to make intercession for us."

In heaven Christ offers himself—once slain, now forever living—to God the Father that men individually may receive the Redemption he won for our race. At Mass, as Catholics believe, the same Christ (through the priest he empowers) offers the same self (really present by the Consecration) to the same heavenly Father, for the same purpose. The Mass is Calvary as Christ now offers it to his Father; and we are given the privilege of joining with Christ in the offering.

The response to this of the group was of two sorts. Those with a devotion to the Mass were glad, it made the

Mass so much more than a "commemorative meal" (surely the most heart-cooling phrase ever invented by cool-hearted men for this ultimate co-operation between Christ and men). But most, I think, were wholly unmoved, and for a reason of horrifying simplicity: Christ Our Lord is no longer sufficiently real to them.

He is a name, a word, an echo from long past. Redemption is hardly even a word, just ten letters. They do not deny Christ, but he is not alive to them. Life as they are involved in it presses in on them inescapably: from Christ they feel no pressure. Life attracts them, frightens them, delights them. Christ has it in him to attract and frighten and delight, as all the Christian centuries have shown: the lives of individuals and of whole societies have been changed by him, but only when he is known. Too often he is "learnt" as one item in a religious syllabus, the pupil getting him as part of a package deal—Christ, his teachings, commands, Church, sacraments—offered as a whole, and increasingly in our day rejected as a whole.

I said at the beginning that the name of the town is irrelevant. It would be rude to say that its name is Legion: but certainly I have had roughly the same experience all over the English-speaking world, in halls and under the open sky, talking with Catholics and Protestants and inter-Faith groups. The religious fact of the moment is what we may call the fading or dimming of Christ in men who sincerely believe in him. Christ is not denied but not much adverted to, not seen as living, present, functioning here and now, not seen as making any noticeable difference. After a talk I gave in Madras, the *Catholic Leader* there called this fading "Sheed's

Disease"—as it might be Parkinson's—because I had isolated and diagnosed it. What the Christ who actually was has to give to men personally and to our own exploding social order must remain locked up in him, unless he is known.

2

We have been considering the dimming of Christ in our generation, the strange phenomenon of Christians who try to live by Christ's standards, would rather die than deny him, yet do not in daily living give very much thought to him, do not seek to meet him very often in the Gospels, and would find it hard to say what *actual difference* his life makes to them or even his death.

How far this is a description of oneself, only oneself can decide. How far it is a description of an attitude to Christ Jesus fairly common among us, that also each of us must decide. It may, of course, be just one man's fancy. But even if it is, how did I arrive at it? Why am I every day more convinced that this phenomenon exists and is growing, that it is the main religious fact of today, the main Christian problem?

In *Is It the Same Church?* I talked of the hymns men used to sing and wondered if we ourselves could sing them—or even, to use a phrase of my son's, say them with our wrist strapped to a lie-detector. "Jesu, joy of man's desiring": Bach's music can still speak to us, but can the words? Those words? When we hear Handel's *Messiah,* we are all vibrant—but are we vibrating to the Messiah, or to Handel, or to the soprano? As a boy I joined lustily in

> How sweet the name of Jesus sounds
> In my enraptured ear;

but in those days the whole point of hymns was in the singing, not the meaning. Had I been questioned I should have admitted no rapture, no excitement at all.

Fashions in speech change. A lover would not today ask a girl to drink to him only with her eyes. But love goes on and is still uttered in love songs. Do we feel, and have we any urge to express in our own terms, any warmth of devotion to Jesus? The question matters profoundly. A line like "What a friend we have in Jesus" is of no high literary value. But if what the words are saying expresses nothing in ourselves, we have lost something vital. Without a sense of our Saviour's personal closeness to us, salvation itself will seem remote and abstract. We must never write off the difference he makes—not solely by what he has done or said but by what he is. Our faith can be no more real to us than he himself. How real is he?

In the world outside, as we meet it in newspapers and on television, his reality seems to be not much emphasized. To the old-style evangelist he was wholly real. But as we read and hear so many present religious leaders we catch no faintest echo of Charles Wesley's "Jesus, lover of my soul, let me to thy bosom fly"; still less of St. Paul's "With Christ I am nailed to the cross." It may be that we are seeing only their public face, that within them there is a Wesley or a Paul struggling to get out. But nothing could be further from personal devotion than what actually reaches us.

I remember the jump I gave the first time I saw our Lord and Saviour referred to as "the Christ Event." I soon got accustomed to the draining off of personality. The Messiah of the Old Testament (and Handel) is treated not as Someone, but as a state of things in which men will live in harmony with one another. So with the Jesus of the New Testament: his life and death and resurrection and ascension add up to a parable. It is not actually denied that it may have happened like that; the question is simply smiled away, as though to think it matters is to miss the point. What matters in a parable is the Meaning—we know Jesus was not talking of a particular prodigal son who ate the husks of particular swine. It is almost a sleight-of-hand trick, this mention of parable. Clearly, if the prodigal son is fiction, we lose nothing. But if Calvary did not happen, we are not redeemed.

It is strange that when all attention is upon Christ's humanity and away from his divinity, his Mother should be so pointedly omitted—Events don't have mothers, nor do Meanings! I mention her here as an illustration of the way in which the atmosphere of our world seeps into us without our noticing. I wonder if that could be the reason why she is not much mentioned among ourselves: I cannot remember when I last heard a sermon about her.

To summarize: awareness of Jesus is a vitalizing principle in Faith. How aware are we? An examination of conscience can be a lacerating experience. It is not our conscience, however, that we are about to examine, but our consciousness, our actual awareness of Christ. That might be lacerating, too.

I have described the incident of hundreds of Catholic high school boys and girls discussing the point of going to Mass, without once mentioning Christ; and indeed, in all the heated arguments we get into about the new Mass rituals, it is rare to find him figuring. This is only one of many matters on which men have managed to stop adverting to him. Take a quick look at another of them.

Priests have been leaving because of the failure of the Institutional Church. In their apologias they tell of its injustice and callousness, of its insensitivity to mankind's real needs. It is odd how seldom they mention Christ, odd how seldom we notice the omission. One is reminded of the scorching attacks made by the prophets on Institutional Israel. Had the prophets and all the holy ones abandoned it, there would have been no Israel left to produce Elizabeth and John the Baptist, Mary and Joseph and Peter and John and Paul, to say nothing of so many magnificent sons of Israel who never found Christ. But it never occurred to the men of virtue to leave. Israel was the People of God, and God was with His People. The running of the Institution might be at any given period in good hands or bad, competent or incompetent: but Institution there had to be; otherwise the treasures of truth and worship entrusted to the People of God would have been left to the mercy of every wind that blew and would soon have been reduced to a chaos of glittering bits and pieces.

We do not belong to the Church because of pope or hierarchy: we may like them or dislike them, but they are not the point. If we think they are handling the Church outrageously, our first instinctive reaction should be grief for Christ whose work they are damaging, whose face they are obscuring. In that feeling we should make our protest—very much as St. John Fisher could say, "If the Pope does not reform the Curia, God will," yet die on the headsman's block for Papal Supremacy.

The trouble is that Popes and Bishops are so spectacularly present, Jesus so quietly. The world does not listen to him. How much listening do we do ourselves? He said scores of things. We remember a sparse handful: "Thou art Peter," "Take up thy bed and walk," "Get thee behind me, Satan" (not always realized as spoken to the miserable Peter), "Whose sins you shall forgive," "My God, my God, why hast thou forsaken me?" Each one of us could add a few more, but what proportion would they bear to the superb mass of even as much as the Gospels record?

He promised to be with us till the world ends, and he wants us to be with him. "Come unto *me,*" he urges, "all you who labor, and I will give you rest." Books or lectures about honesty in the Church tend to be about the dishonesty of our leaders. But what matters most to our individual selves is our own honesty, that we should not be fooling ourselves—deceiving others is sin, deceiving ourselves is insanity. Christ wants our company. *Do we want his?*

The Church, I have noted, can fill our horizon to the exclusion of its Founder. The world can block out both. The Church used to understand the value of reminders, words or acts that could make him suddenly present in a distracting world—crucifixes, ejaculatory prayers, meatless Fridays, confession, visits to the Blessed Sacrament (I never come away from a visit without feeling, in that moment, closer to him). But basic to them all, releasing their full power to help, is personal knowledge of Jesus himself.

Most of us, I fancy, still feel that we ought to know the Christ of Galilee and Judea better than we do. We make fitful resolutions to do some serious Gospel reading, as we make fitful resolutions to reduce our weight. But a new sound is heard among us—the Christ of the Gospels is all very well, we hear, but he was two thousand years ago: what matters to me is seeing Christ in my fellow man. One sometimes wonders what the words are saying. If they mean that we treat even one of our fellows as though he were Christ, it is a vast commitment of love and service. But, even at that, surely we should be better equipped to recognize Christ as he meets us in others by knowing him as he was in himself.

3

Let us linger a while on the notion, proclaimed by so many as today's discovery, that our duty as Christians is to find Jesus not in the Gospels but in our fellow men, especially in the poor and the suffering.

What is positive in it is not today's discovery, of course, precious fruit of Vatican II. We meet it all down the ages. No one has put it better than William Langland in his *Vision of Piers Plowman:*

> Jesus Christ of heaven
> In the apparel of a poor man pursues us always.

Langland came six hundred years too soon to get that from Vatican II.

It goes right back, of course, to Jesus himself, which makes it all the stranger that it should be proposed as an alternative to the Gospel Jesus. Read the last dozen verses of Matthew's chapter 25. Try reading them as if we had never read them before, shaking free of the pious coma which is our ordinary tribute to Scripture's sacredness. If, Christ says, we do not feed the hungry, give drink to the thirsty, clothe the naked, visit the sick or imprisoned, it is Christ himself to whom we are refusing food, drink, clothing, comfort. It is one sin he actually names as leading to everlasting punishment, just as the reverse is the way to everlasting life. From the beginning of the world no religious founder had ever thus identified either God or himself with the neediest.

I have heard it said, rather superiorly, that giving food to a starving man does not solve the national problem of malnutrition. By all means work at the solution of the larger problem, but do not downgrade those who actually put food into hungry mouths. They are very close to the Jesus of Lazarus whom Dives ignored, the Jesus of the Good Samaritan. My wife wonders if the priest and Levite were too deeply occupied with the problem of Safety on the Roads to bother about the wounded man: perhaps they were: but Jesus found them un-neighborly, the Samaritan is his hero.

Our overall question in this book is the difference Jesus made. His teaching in this field is different; taken seriously, it could change the world. And it has made a difference—not all the difference, unfortunately, but vast. At every level there have been Christians who acted differently because of it; it has spread to a world that hardly knows Christ, so profound a nerve it touches in men.

I say that it has not made all the difference. We are back at the pious coma in which we do so much of our Scripture reading and Scripture listening. Even in coma we cannot fail to realize that we are being urged to give to the needy and we dutifully do; but we hardly notice that salvation or damnation is involved: our complacency is not penetrated by the realization that if we refuse, we are refusing Christ! Giving some of what we happen to have left over after suitably affluent living— that is hardly what Christ could have meant by feeding the hungry as if they were himself.

And there is a danger for ourselves in this talk of seeing Christ in our fellow men. It can too easily become a sort of slogan or catchword, the words formed in the mouth, not in the mind. What the words are saying is indeed so vast a commitment—that we should love others as we should love Christ, serve them as we would serve Christ! The phrase is uttered so lightly: one wonders if the needy always feel that those who utter it are treating them as Christ!

A further question arises: when we see Christ in others, what are we seeing? How do we in fact see Christ? Pretty variously. When the mind has not been brought fully into action listening and responding, he is sometimes scaled down to a single quality, kindness— he was fond of children, merciful to sinners, wept over dead Lazarus. I call this scaling down, not because kindness is not a splendid quality, but because so many other qualities are left out that even his love is not seen aright. There is his strength, for instance, his curtness of speech and complete absence of sentimentality, his insistence upon our keeping the commandments if we are to inherit eternal life, the power of his rage, the occasional invective ("the harlots shall enter the kingdom of heaven before you").

Basing everything on love, reduced thus to kindness, can produce improbable results—I know of a man who left wife and children in poverty, persuaded a nun to leave her convent and live with him: he and the nun are daily communicants, convinced they are living up to Christ's command of love. One imagines they make their own accommodation with his statement that adultery defiles.

There is another way of seeing Christ—as a piece in the theological diagram of redemption, an automaton moving majestically on a path decided for him by his heavenly Father and blueprinted for him by the prophets, himself hardly reacting until what looks like a momentary breakdown in the Garden of Olives.

Both these ways of seeing him assume that he had not only a soul that was for all practical purposes divine, but a perfect body fresh-minted for himself. It is time we met the Jesus that actually was. In the Gospels, of course. Where else?

4

That very notable Irish leader Eamonn de Valera is said to have said, "When I want to know what Ireland wants, I look into my own heart." One's instant comment is "Why not ask Ireland?" At the present time too many Catholics seem to be finding what Christ wants by looking into their own hearts, instead of meeting him and listening to him in the Gospels. There is where he is to be met as he lived and moved, died and rose: there, nowhere else. It is easy to invent one's own Christ, or one's own Ireland for that matter, out of one's own best self; but as a way of treating Ireland it would not make much sense: as a way of treating Christ it is pathetic beyond all reason.

Live with the Gospels, then. And by the Gospels I do not mean what's left of them when the latest critic has put his knife back into its sheath. I mean Matthew, Mark, Luke and John, as men have seen the face of Christ in them through nineteen centuries. When you have really lived with what's there, you can learn from the critics but you will not be at their mercy, for you will have your own personal knowledge of Christ and your own individual reaction—not to the Christ Event, but to Jesus of Nazareth. With that knowledge you can consider what the theologians and the Scripture scholars have for your profit.

One hears it said that the very first Christians were interested only in the Message, the Event—and that interest in the personality of Christ, and therefore the Gospel accounts of what he said and did, came only later. If so, if they did not beg those who knew him to tell them about him, then in their lack of interest in a hero recently dead for whom they themselves might be called upon to die, they must have been unlike any human beings that ever lived. Of the first Christians, I simply do not believe it. But, as we have noted, it is a fair description of many Christians, ourselves included, nineteen hundred years later.

If he continues to fade into the background, his message will not last: its power upon men has always lain in its being his—not so many words on a page, but words they hear issuing from the mouth of him who was scourged and thorn-crowned and crucified and in agony pleaded for God's forgiveness for his torturers. It is not the truths we take into ourselves, but himself with the truths adhering. He, not his teaching by itself, has brought men to heroism. This being so, the first gift we seek from the Gospels is growth in intimacy with him: the rest depends upon that. A great sermon may set us vibrating—to the preacher. We must have our own vibration to Christ. Without that, reading books on the love of Christ is like reading someone else's love letters.

Chapter II

A Man but Different

I

Taking the Gospels as we find them, we see Jesus as at once clearly man and clearly different. We must linger on both clarities.

Man first. I have said that there has been a tendency among men genuinely devout to think of him in his humanity as all but God. They know he had a human mind, of course. The Church has had to answer heretics who questioned the humanness of his intellect, and others who asserted that at least the will was divine not human. The Church's answer can be put in all terseness —if he hadn't a human intellect and a human will he would not have been man. The last-ditchers compromised by calling his human intellect and will practically divine, quasi-infinite: there was his knowledge, for instance—though as man he was not omniscient, there was nothing he did not know!

There was not the same tendency to see his body as infinite—bodies cannot be, and in any event he experienced birth, hunger and thirst, suffering and death. But there has been the assumption already referred to —that his body was perfect, fresh-minted for him. To this also the Church replies that if that were so he would not have been a man. And a man he was. He did not take on human nature in the abstract but this particular human nature. He did not become man in general, he became this particular man. He was a true member of our race.

We get our bodies from an uncountable number of ancestors—back fourteen hundred generations at least, maybe fourteen thousand. So did Christ. He was the fruit of David's loins, says Peter; of the seed of David according to the flesh, says Paul. And David was a good forty generations back. Christ's body was not fresh-minted for him. The body he had to live with, in which he had to redeem us, was the body he got from a myriad of ancestors going back to the beginning of the human race.

To the Christ of the Gospels everyone must have his own reaction. There are those who reject both him and the Gospels in one inclusive sweep. Of those who do not, I fancy that most see him as I have just described him, at once definitely man and quite certainly different from any other man known to history. Today still, as through the centuries, the differences cause people to feel that to call him man and leave it at that leaves out too much—in some way he is Man Plus. But what does the Plus stand for?

To vast numbers it is Divinity, Christ is the God-Man, whether they believe him both God and Man, or only a man uniquely indwelt by God, inspired by God as no other man has been. Those who overrate the differences write his manhood down, even write it off as a mask the Divine chose to wear, a tool It chose to use. Those who underrate the differences may find themselves left with a rather improbable man, with whom there can be no warmth of feeling and no urge to a personal relation, one who too easily becomes the Christ Event.

Before we try to evaluate the differences, let us take a long look at them. For the moment I am not thinking of special occasions—his birth of a Virgin Mother (told us by Matthew and Luke), his Miracles, Transfiguration, Calvary, Resurrection and Ascension—but of what we may call his ordinary way of speaking of himself in relation to men and to God. The unvarying element in this is his assumption of something special in himself, something not in other men unless he gives it to them.

"Come unto me all you who labor and are heavily burdened and I will give you rest" (Matthew 11.28)—as heart-warming a phrase as any God spoke to men in the Psalms. But there was another edge to his "difference." "He who loves father or mother more than me is not worthy of me" (Matthew 10.37) is a saying clearly monstrous if he is man and no more: even some of those who accept his Godhead find it hard to fit it into their picture of him.

What the crowd felt at the end of the Sermon on the Mount his close followers knew from daily experience —"the crowds were astonished at his teaching, for he taught them as one who has authority and not as their scribes" (Matthew 8.9). Later he was to give the Apostles commands meant for the whole world—"Going teach all nations, teaching them to observe all things whatsoever I have commanded you" (Matthew 20.7). Thus he spoke to those who had already accepted him. But the Sermon on the Mount (Matthew 5 to 7) was for all and sundry. The opening words, "I have come not to destroy the law and the prophets but to fulfill them," you and I can take calmly. But no one in his audience had ever

heard words so shocking and shattering. The Law had been given them by God through Moses (there was one theory that God Himself studied it daily). And here was this nobody from Nazareth promising not to destroy it! His promise to fulfil it was, if anything, more blasphemous. And that was what he set about doing.

He began with three of the Ten Commandments—do not kill, commit adultery, swear falsely. He prefaces each with "It was said to them of old"—i.e., by God through Moses. He follows each with "But I say to you," and develops the command richly, on his own authority, not as a scribe might on the authority of Moses. He goes on to two other great words given by Moses outside the Decalogue. The first is "An eye for an eye and a tooth for a tooth": the Pharisees had already modified this, but Christ goes far beyond, all the way to "Do not refuse him who would borrow from you"! The second is "You shall love your neighbor as yourself"—one of his "developments" here is one of the greatest things ever said: "Love your enemies, pray for those that persecute you." Anyone who feels he has outgrown Christ might try outgrowing that. (I remember the reaction of an outdoor crowd in New York's Times Square, ranging from speechless indignation to obscenity, when I asked if they would pray for Hitler.)

He never speaks of apostles or anyone else as his equals. The authority he claims is total. But it is not his. It comes from his Father: "As my Father appointed a kingdom to me, so do I appoint for you" (Luke 22.29). Basic to his whole life was his certainty of a special relation to God. Illusion? But how reconcile that illusion with the electrifying sanity of so much else that he said?

2

To write off Christ's certainty about himself as a delusion of grandeur or any sort of megalomania is difficult for one who really reads the Gospels, meeting the astonishing assertions of his relation to God in their context as he says them. The nine beatitudes at the beginning of the Sermon on the Mount (Ma.thew 5) sum up the rule of human life so profoundly that men of other religions and men of no religion at all find joy in them. In that same sermon are other phrases which have become mankind's possession, phrases such as no religious fanatic ever uttered. Not only "Love your enemies," but "Consider the lilies of the field," "You cannot serve God and mammon," "By their fruits you shall know them," "Do unto others as you would want them to do to you," "Judge not that you be not judged," the Lord's Prayer with its "Forgive us our trespasses *as we forgive.*"

So delusion, illusion, will not do as an explanation. But explanation is called for. And for most of his three years he himself seemed more bent on emphasizing the mystery than explaining it. Take the phrase he, and only he, used of himself—the Son of Man. You will find it eighty times in the Gospels. But his followers never use it; and after the Gospels it practically vanishes— occurring only once, in Stephen's vision before his stoning (Acts 6). Clearly, to Christ's first followers it answered no question, it only indicated that there was a question to answer. It tantalized them, it tantalized the crowd—"Who is this son of man?" they asked him, and got no reply. It has tantalized men ever since—unnecessarily, as I think.

In itself, "son of man" was only a way of saying

"man." Throughout Ezekiel, God uses it thus a hundred times or so in addressing the prophet. Once only the Old Testament has it memorably. In Daniel (8.13) the prophet describes a vision: "With the clouds of heaven came one like a Son of Man [i.e., with the appearance of a man, not an angel] . . . and he came to the Ancient of Days and was presented before him. And to him was given dominion and glory and a kingdom, that all peoples should serve him, his dominion is everlasting." This is, I have said, the one memorable use of the phrase in Scripture; but the apocalyptic books 4 Esdras and Enoch, written between the two Testaments, made much of it—Enoch speaking of a Son of Man hidden from the beginning. And the Daniel passage was clearly in Christ's own mind. When Caiphas the High Priest asked him if he was "the Christ, the Son of God" (Peter's phrase), he said, "Hereafter you shall see the Son of Man . . . coming on the clouds of heaven" (Matthew 26.57). And the words about "all peoples" and "everlasting dominion" are echoed in his command to his apostles to teach all nations and his promise to be with them all days even to the end of the world (Matthew 28).

But I think there is another reason for his choice of phrase. After all, between "the Son of Man" and "a being like a son of man" there is a vast difference. We must not exaggerate the word "the," but we cannot overlook it. Christ is calling himself The Man, which is what chapters 2 and 3 of Genesis call our first parent. "The Adam" means "the man": not until chapter 4 is Adam used as his name. Jesus seems clearly to be asserting that he was the first man of a new humanity, as Adam of the old. Paul was to work this out in his teaching on the Second Adam, but it is already there.

As Son of Man, Christ added to the shocks his hearers might have received from the Sermon on the Mount. With "The son of man has power on earth to forgive sins" (Matthew 9.6), he claims a power reserved in the Old Testament entirely to God. "The Son of Man is Lord of the Sabbath" must have been, verbally, more startling than anything I have yet quoted: however lax a Jew might have been, the Sabbath was one observance he never dropped: the Romans had to stop conscripting Jews because their "Sabbath rest" made things too complicated for their officers. You might almost say that the Sabbath *was* Judaism: and they believed that God Himself observed it.

But in Matthew 11 and Luke 10 we find him claiming for himself another Sonship, compared with which Son of Man is a trifle. I quote from Luke: "All things have been delivered to me by my Father; and no one knows the Son except the Father, and no one knows the Father except the Son and anyone to whom the Son chooses to reveal him." Christ is asserting a unique equality of inter-knowledge between his Father and himself, each knowing the other as no one beside knows either. There is no hint here of inequality, nor yet the air of one saying something that has never been said before, something that could be explained only by being explained away. It all flows from him so naturally. It is just what we might have expected to find in John. But it is given us by Matthew and Luke. We have not yet drawn upon John. We are not quite ready for John yet.

3

Through the ages there has been a tendency among those who love Jesus to concentrate on, and magnify, the differences between him and other men to the point where his humanness hardly matters. No heresy has a more continuous appeal to the devout than the earliest of all, Docetism, with its teaching that his human body was only a phantom.

The tendency is the other way today. Yet there are still those who see any serious emphasis on his manhood and its limitations as a denial of his diviniⅼy. There is a simplification in *either* man *or* God that only heads clear enough for the rich complexity of *both* man *and* God can avoid.

We begin with the error already referred to—that his body was new-made for him with all the perfections a human body can have. This would mean that his body was not conceived by Mary, but that an embryo, not drawn from her body but created by God independently of it, was placed in her womb that it might make use of the womb's facilities for the necessary nine months (there were indeed early heretics who held this). She would have been the baby's hostess, not his mother.

Against this stand the statements of Matthew and Luke that she conceived him. Peter has told us that he was the fruit of David's loins (Acts 2.30), Paul that he was of the seed of David according to the flesh. So, naturally, was his mother. She received Sanctifying Grace, the Church has defined, at the moment of her conception: but this did not replace her genes and chromosomes. Christ's ancestry then, like ours, goes back to the origin of the human race. He got his body, as we get ours, from a myriad ancestors—back 35,000 years? 350,000? how many? This, as we have already noted, was the body in which he died for our redemption and rose again. More to our present purpose, it was the body he had to live with, to cope with: the cross often enough that he had to carry, as we have to carry ours.

In it was a vast complexity of inherited instincts and tendencies. As a result there would be actions that came easy to him and others he found difficult, responses that came automatically and responses that had to be thought out, things that attracted him and things that repelled him and things that meant nothing either way. What did temptation mean to him?

Hebrews (4.15) says that he was "able to sympathize with our weakness" because he was tempted as we are in all things but did not sin. That word "tempted" could mislead us. Our modern use of it emphasizes *our* reaction—only if we find ourselves desiring to do something we feel we oughtn't, do we say that we are tempted. But as used in Scripture, temptation emphasizes what the tempter offers, whether or not men are attracted. There is not a hint that he found any attraction in Satan's temptations in the desert: the episode tells us more about Satan than about Jesus. In our present text the Jerusalem Bible translates that he was *"tested in all things as we are."* The world, the flesh and the devil offered the same possibilities of pleasure in sin to him as to us.

Hebrews says he did not sin. He himself had uttered the challenge "Who shall convict me of sin?" And he had stated as the rule of his life: "My will is to do the will of him that sent me": and sin is the choice of our own will as against the order of reality as God has made it. So he did not yield to temptation. But was he tempted in our sense, was he drawn to desire, or at least to feel the attraction of, what would have been sin had he yielded? Those with strong views can say "Of course he was" (or "wasn't" if that's how they see it). We can speculate like this but we cannot know.

Of what value is our speculation? We have a nodding acquaintance with how a human body and a human will can act when these are our own (though at that we can surprise ourselves). We can make a reasonably good guess about the temptations and decisions of other people (but again and again our guess is wrong). The person—that in each of us which says "I"—is beyond our gaze. And this must be far more so when the person is divine. We can arrive at a sort of statistical average about people in general. But we cannot strike that sort of average about God-men because there has been only one of them.

What temptation meant within him we can know only if he tells us, and he does not—not at least in regard to the ordinary daily temptations. There was indeed one crisis point. In Gethsemane he cried, "Father, if it is your will, remove this cup [of suffering] from me; nevertheless *not my will but yours be done"* (Luke 22.39).

4

There is only one virtue we are told Christ had to learn. If we had not read Hebrews, would we guess that it was obedience? Obedience it was, but the writer of Hebrews cannot conceal his own surprise: *"Though he was Son,* he learned obedience through what he suffered" (5.8). What was there for him to learn?

In Gethsemane Jesus asked his Father to save him from drinking the cup of redemptive suffering (Luke 22.42); but he followed that cry of anguish with "Nevertheless not my will but yours be done." Was that the first time these words were ever drawn from him, or wrenched from him, the first time he had to make the effort to harmonize his will with his Father's? Gethsemane was a climax: but had there been earlier moments when his No to the pleasure disobedience offered, or his Yes to the pain obedience must bring with it, was not simply automatic? Unless he tells us, we can only speculate. But Hebrews itself seems to guide our speculation: "Because he himself has suffered and been tempted, he is able to help those who are tempted" (2.18); and "he is able to sympathize with our weaknesses because he has been tempted as we are, even though he did not sin" (4.15).

Unless he tells us, I have just said. He tells us so little of his own mind, will, emotions. And even that little we can miss if we are not wholly concentrated on what the Gospels are saying. Consider two earlier passages whose link with the cry in Gethsemane we may have overlooked.

Once only he speaks of an impatience personal to himself. "I have a baptism to be baptized with, and how I am constrained until it is accomplished" (Luke 12.50). He was speaking of the bathing in his own blood on Calvary. Knowledge of the agony he must undergo for mankind's redemption was always with him, and he found the waiting hard to bear. He was longing for it to happen and be over. Yet when the happening was upon him, he cried to his Father to spare him from it! The Gospels are difficult to read. So is Christ. This incident illustrates both difficulties.

Consider another. He had told the Apostles how he must suffer and be killed in Jerusalem and on the third day be raised (Matthew 16.21). Peter, making nothing of the raising but finding unbearable the suffering and slaying of the Lord he loved, protested that it must not happen. Christ answered, "Get thee behind me, Satan." Peter's failure to understand needed correction, of course, as when later he drew his sword at Christ's arrest. Yet we are startled at the vehemence, the almost ferocity of calling him Satan.

But have we noticed that in Gethsemane Our Lord sounds as if he were asking his Father to do for him what he had called Satanic when Peter had urged it upon himself? It means that Peter's urging had set a nerve throbbing in his Lord, an anticipation of the moment in Gethsemane when "his soul was sorrowful even unto death" (Mark 14.34).

Christ *is* hard for us to read. Yet the effort is immeasurably worth making. Unless he is alive to us, his message will not be. We must look long at his humanity before we can see what meaning there is for us in his divinity.

That Christ is indeed man no one reading the Gospels can doubt: even if we see him as Man Plus, the plus does not eliminate the man. Yet at one point it almost seems to. I mean his sinlessness. Sin we find so easy, so effortless, that it is hard to think of one who never sinned as completely human. "To err is human," said that not very ardent Catholic poet, Alexander Pope. But Christ did not err, so——

No only for the understanding of his life, but for the running of our own, it will repay us to linger upon this. It is true that sin, deliberately doing what we know is wrong, is possible to humans as it is not to animals. But all the same sin is not a way of being human, sin is a way of misusing our humanity, it is a diminution of manhood, not a completion. The comparison with disease is exact. It is probably true that there has never been a man without some bodily defect. But if there were such a man he would not be less than human. Christ was tempted in all things as we are. He was more of a man for not yielding.

How far was his sinlessness simply a result of his divinity? We are close to the heart of what it means to be a God-man—what it can mean to us who try to understand it, what it must have meant to him who had to be it.

Chapter III

Jesus as Men Met Him

Thou hast conquered, O pale Galilean; the world has
grown grey from Thy breath. . . .

No one who knows anything of the world into which
Christ came would regard it as of a lovely greenness
shrivelled to grey by him. It was a world bathed in blood,
shot through with misery, melancholy at its gayest. Matthew's words "They were harassed and helpless like
sheep without a shepherd" (9.36) were a precise description not only of the crowds on whom Jesus gazed com-
passionately, but of the whole of that world. Indeed it
would be hard to think up a better ten-word description
of people today, just about anywhere—"harassed and
helpless like sheep without a shepherd."

Yet men, even great masses of Christian men, do not
turn to him or even think of him. There are two reasons
for this. Since people do not see themselves as they are,
he meets no needs they actually feel (that being their
test of relevance). Neither do they see Jesus as *he* is.
How are we to bring into contact the unrealized needs
and the ill-known Jesus?

It is not enough to study his teachings, we must be in
contact with himself. So we look more closely, not at
the "Christ Event," not at the "Myth," but at Jesus of

Nazareth. Is kindness the whole of him, do "gentle,"
"meek," "mild" convey him adequately?

We are sometimes told with surprise that he kept
company with tax collectors and sinners. But surely
what is surprising is that they wanted his company—
such people are pretty choosy, not ready to be bored. All
the same the Gospels are not a textbook on How to Win
Friends. With individuals his speech is terse, with no
words wasted and no sentimentality. He was sparing of
praise, for instance: four or five people he praises,
briefly; and only one of these was (but not yet) an Apostle—Nathanael, "an Israelite without guile." Then there
is the pagan centurion—"I have not found such faith in
Israel"; a scribe—"you are not far from the kingdom"
(Mark 12.34, not very exuberant, that); Mary of Bethany
—"she has chosen the better part"; and John the Baptist
—"no man born of woman is greater than he."

He had compassion on crowds, but not much is re-
counted of his love for individuals. We are told he loved
"his own [the Apostles] to the end"; loved Martha and
her sister and Lazarus, loved the rich young man who
rejected his call.

"I call you friends," he says to the Apostles. But we
only hear him address one man as "Friend," namely
Judas, in the moment of betrayal—"Friend, what have
you come for?" No scholar has yet used this as proof that
he regarded Judas as his only friend, but I know some
who would if it supported some theory of their own. I am
reminded of an old No Popery objection against Our
Lady—"Christ never called her Mother." Nor indeed is
there any record of his doing so. But we hear him speak
to her only three times all told, and even the most filial
of sons does not put "Mother" into every sentence. I

remember on one occasion retorting, "We never hear that she called him Jesus, either. So what?" As it happens, only three times in the Gospels do we hear him addressed as Jesus—by a demon he was casting out, by some lepers, and by blind Bartimeus at Jericho.

I use these trifles as a reminder that no argument can be built on what is *not* in the Gospels—he may have praised lots of people, loved lots of people, called lots of people friend. But there remain the things the Gospels do have him saying. One remembers the hymn line "How beautiful are gentle words and loving smiles." From Jesus we hear some not very gentle words.

To Peter, urging him not to go to Jerusalem to suffer and die, he said, "Get thee behind me, Satan." When the Gentile woman wanted him to heal her daughter he asked her if she expected him to take the bread of the children—the Chosen People—and give it to dogs (Matthew 15; in case you don't remember, he did heal the daughter). To those who followed him to Capharnaum after the miracle of loaves and fishes he said, "You're here because I fed you." Even the beloved disciple heard strong rebuke: when he and his brother James wanted Jesus to bring down fire on the Samaritan cities which had rejected him, he told them: "You do no know of what spirit you are. I have come to save not to destroy" (Luke 9.55).

I have listed some ungentle words. What about loving smiles? We are not told that he or any other New Testament character laughed or smiled. At many points we may imagine him as doing one or the other: one hardly imagines his as the only grave face at the wedding in Cana. But at the beginning of his public life he spoke of the death he must die (John 3.14). He walked in the shadow of that.

What would be the effect of a visit by Christ Our Lord to your town or my town or anybody's town today? If we are to believe John Lennon, he had better not come while the Beatles are in town, because they have more crowd appeal than he ever had. That was said a year or so ago and there are already signs that the Beatle influence may not last as long as Christ's. In any event crowds are not the point of my question, but what we— you and I and everybody—would really make of him. How would what *he* has to offer appeal to *us*?

What put the title of the chapter into my head was the remembrance of a forty-year-back article in a London daily paper, under the heading "If Christ Came to London." It was all about the people Christ would scourge as he scourged the money changers, and a vast number they proved to be. But the writer did not list himself among them—clearly he saw himself going around with Christ drawing his attention to any scourgeables he was in danger of overlooking. Within a short time the writer was co-respondent in a divorce case. He clearly had forgotten, if he had ever known, that Christ had listed adultery among the sins that defile a man (Matthew 15.18–20), or perhaps, like the couple I spoke of earlier, he had his own interpretation of it. I mention the matter as an example of what could happen on our imaginary visit—many might find the real Christ a shock after the rather filleted Christ which is all that remains in their memories after too long an abstinence from Gospel reading.

The reporters who met him on arrival would find him as unpleasing as the scribes of his own day, for a different reason, of course: whereas the scribes found him heretical, the reporters would find him uncooperative—terse, no small talk, no jokes, no comments on the political situation. The Romans held his country by the throat, but he joined no Palestine Liberation Front. Only "Render unto Caesar the things that are Caesar's" (Matthew 22.21). How could anybody make a headline of that?

The reporters would go their bored way and leave him to the public; and many of the public—I mean his own public, the Christians—would find him hard to take. Particularly hard would be his unworldliness. This had been no problem to them when read placidly as texts of Scripture, but very disturbing to placidity as uttered by him, there, looking at them: they might feel a little of what Peter felt after his denial when "Jesus looked at him" (Luke 22.61).

Just as our Christian co-respondent was untroubled by his words on adultery, so most of us would find we had not been troubled enough by his condemnation of the worldliness in which we had wrapped ourselves so comfortably. We had read in Matthew's Gospel that we must feed the hungry and clothe the naked—and we had felt that we had not been lacking in a reasonable generosity with our money and even, perhaps, with our time. But certain words our eyes have glided over—that we must do these things as if the hungry and the naked were Christ himself, and that any failure in all this could mean damnation. We could not be so sure of ourselves, with him standing there saying them, looking at us.

"You cannot serve God and money," we read (Matthew 6.24). Our happy confidence that we have in fact served both would not long survive our hearing the words from him. We should be as embarrassed to have our unbelieving friends hear them as were the Apostles at his saying that if we do not eat his flesh and drink his blood we shall not have life in us.

The examples I have given would trouble his Christian hearers; the rest would dismiss them as nonsense and go back to the Beatles. But there are things he said which even some of the Christians would regard as carrying unworldliness beyond sane limits, and taking otherworldliness more for granted than is our habit: "If your eye or hand or foot causes you to sin, cut off the hand or foot, pluck out the eye. It is better to enter life with one of each than to be cast into hell for ever with two" (Matthew 18.8–10). They feel he could not have meant it literally. But how *did* he mean it? They value his insights, of course, but sayings like this they scale down in terms of reality, realism being their own special gift. The trouble about this sort of evasion is that when he does talk of this world it is with a realism no one has ever matched.

Clearly we need to look at Jesus more closely, listen to him more attentively. He will not come to our town. But we can see him, hear him, in Capharnaum, Bethany, Jerusalem.

He may have surprises for us.

2

After our brief excursion into fantasy, we return to first-century Palestine. What was Christ like to meet? More basically, what sort of man was he? If we are serious about him, we should surely study his character at least as closely as a reader might study the character of Hamlet, whose father willed him to kill, as Christ's Father willed him to die.

But *had* Jesus a character in that sense? And if he

had, is there any point in studying it? At both ends, the ultra-liberal and the ultra-conservative, there are those who would say No.

For too many critics Jesus is nothing but a Meaning or a Message—not Jesus the Carpenter, but the Jesus Event. Above all not the Jesus Fact—its earthiness might adulterate the Meaning, flaw its purity. That was behind the warning we hear against "Jesusolatry"! And indeed many a theory about him could not live with the fact of him.

There is something of this shying away from Jesus of Nazareth in quite orthodox Christians: they remind us that it is the Risen Christ who matters to us now. But the Jesus now in heaven is not another man but that man: and whereas Jesus of Palestine is under our gaze in the Gospels, the Risen Christ is beyond our gaze—so that he is at the mercy of the scholar's speculation with no present fact to check it.

At the other extreme there are the mass of believers to whom the sort of discussion I propose is wholly unreal. They see Jesus not as a man but as a model. They see him as confronted with no choices, because only the perfect was possible to him, and to any situation there was only one perfect response, which came automatically from the union in him of manhood and godhead. Yet in the Garden of his agony he prayed that his Father's will might be done and not his own!

We have talked of this already. Here we merely remind ourselves that in Paul's phrase he was "of the seed of David according to the flesh," that, as Peter put it, he was "the fruit of David's loins." His body came to him immediately from his mother, ultimately from her myriad ancestors back to man's beginning. This body had its own impulses and tendencies. There were things it found desirable and things repulsive, actions that came naturally and actions that could only be carried through with sweat and straining—and this not simply because of the things and actions in themselves, but because of the body he individually had got, as we get ours, from such a variety of ancestors.

When this is not realized, Jesus has to be seen as doing passionlessly what had to be done, himself above the storm. Read his judgment of the Pharisees in chapter 23 of St. Matthew's Gospel, the highest level of sustained invective in all literature. I remember being criticized for speaking of his "rage," it being held irreverent to speak of the God-man as in a rage—apparently he was simply cataloguing the wickednesses of the Pharisees with clinically exact justice.

But he himself has given us the command "Be angry and sin not" (a very difficult combination, as we all realize when we have cooled down after anger). Read Matthew 23 again. You will see the faces, arrogant, sneering. So did he. And to have looked on the wrongs they were doing with no emotional stirring would have been not more human but less. He did not sin, and his anger was enormous. It was hot anger, cold anger is likelier to be sinful.

In the Gospels we can, if we will, meet Jesus for ourselves. Remember what they are, four accounts of the Redeemer, all four coming to their climax in his redeeming action— Passion, Death, Resurrection. One fourth of their ninety or so chapters are given to a single week, from Palm Sunday to Easter. That is the Good News, that is their topic. Building up to the week of Man's Redemption they treat of the couple of years of

Christ's Public Ministry, selecting episodes suited to their purpose in writing. Matthew prefaces his Gospel, as does Luke, with a swift glance at the Conception, Birth and Infancy.

In the Gospels we meet Jesus, and nowhere else—even on the road to Damascus it was unmistakably the Jesus of the Gospels that Paul met. A non-Gospel Jesus is a mere artifact. The art with which it is made may be considerable, but the artist has made it out of his own principles, insights, preferences, prejudices.

But is the Gospel Jesus an artifact too? Was he "created" by the Early Church out of the Carpenter of Nazareth as some think Plato created Socrates out of the bibulous husband of Xantippe?

3

For Jesus as a figure in history we have a handful of statements by pagans. Tacitus, for instance, the greatest of all Roman historians, says in his *Annals* that Pontius Pilate put him to death. But was he simply the raw material which the meditation of the early Church worked up into the Jesus of the Gospels?

In the sense that by receiving him in the Eucharist, living his teachings, thinking about them, praying about them, his followers grew to see deeper meanings and openings to future meanings in his words and actions, this is simply a truth crudely stated. What he left with them did not lie dead in inert minds. But at its extreme point it amounts to the assertion that the Gospel Christ was the invention of his first followers.

The theory is that after his death his hard-core followers did not disband, but continued to meet and to draw others to them. Gradually they developed certain institutional structures, ways of explaining Jesus, forms of worship: then they invented things he was supposed to have said and done which would justify the structures, the interpretations, the rituals.

If you call this fraud, conspiracy to deceive, you will be accused of judging another age by the literary standards of our own. But we are not discussing literature, our concern is with reality. Whether the "inventors" of the Gospel Christ were honest or dishonest, deceivers of others or self-deceived—that was between them and God, and they made their settlement with him long ago. But what value should we attach to their inventions, however excusable? What of reality is left to us?

We must take a very long look at all this later. But for our present purpose it does not much signify. As used, it is a way of writing off Christ's divinity, his relations to his Father and the Holy Spirit, his miracles, and any teachings particular critics feel that as modern men they cannot swallow—angels for instance, hell, a teaching Church. In a general way it is a stripping away of God's interventions in the life of Jesus and in the life of men. But it does not cast doubt on the words and deeds which reveal his human character, the sort of man he was, the man friends and enemies actually met. To meet him thus is our present concern.

What no one questions is his hostility to the Establishment, and this is all in his favor today when Establishment is a very dirty word indeed.

The Establishment in Palestine was not one single simple system. There was the Political regime, entirely under the control of Rome. Pontius Pilate was the Roman procurator of Judea. There were various kinglets, like Herod the Great: towards the end of his life Jesus was born. His son Herod Antipas, ruling in Galilee, stole his brother Philip's wife, beheaded John the Baptist who had criticized him for it, had a small part in the trial of Jesus. A nephew, Herod Agrippa, beheaded James, the first Apostle to be martyred. They were great beheaders, these Herods: but they cringed before the Roman Emperor, as did Pontius Pilate.

Our Lord seems to have bothered little with the Political Establishment. His war was with the religious leaders. Within Jewry there were two main divisions, Sadducees and Pharisees, fiercely hostile. Reading the Gospels, we hear most about the Pharisees, strict legalists, strict ritualists. The Sadducees differed mainly by accepting only the first five books of the Bible as binding: the Pharisees held these books above the rest, but accepted also the Historical Books, the Psalms, the Prophets: not only that, they studied the commentaries of the learned men, the scribes. The Pharisees in short held that God had not said his last word to mankind thirteen hundred years before in the Sinai desert—the word God spoke to their immaturity might not be the whole of his word for them now.

Their hostility to the Sadducees had another element. The Sadducees were a rich aristocracy, hand in glove with the pagan Romans. As a result they had the Temple and the High Priesthood and the Temple Treasury. They were essentially worldly men, which may have been why the denial of any life after this suited them.

With all their accumulated hatreds, the Sadducees led by Caiphas the High Priest had the Pharisees with them in pressuring the Roman procurator to crucify Jesus. Ironically, a few years later the fourth of Caiphas' brothers to be appointed High Priest by Rome was stabbed to death by a very extremist Pharisee. And forty years after the Crucifixion, Rome destroyed Jerusalem, Temple and all, and with it the sons of those who cried out that they had no king but Caesar. But for the moment they were united in wanting Christ killed. He spent the whole of his public life in the certainty that he would be.

After Peter's profession of faith in Jesus as Son of the Living God (Matthew 16.16, Mark 8.29), we find Jesus telling the Twelve that he must go to Jerusalem, suffer at the hands of chief priests and scribes, and be killed. Peter begs him not to, is called Satan for his pains, and all of them hear the warning to themselves: "If any would come after me, let him take up his cross and follow me."

In the week that ended with his Crucifixion, he said: "I, when I am lifted up from the earth, will draw all men to me" (John 12.32). Somewhere I have read that "lifted up" was a colloquial phrase for crucifixion, as in England "swing" is to to hanged, in America to "burn" is to be electrocuted. However that may be, John adds that Jesus used the phrase to "show by what death he must die."

How early do the Gospels show him as knowing the agony to come? From the beginning of his public ministry, certainly. Immediately after Cana, he delivered his first challenge to the Establishment, scattering the money-changers in the Temple courtyard with a whip (John 2.13) for making his Father's house a den of thieves. Immediately after that we meet "lifted up" for the first time (John 3.14). In conversation with Nicodemus, a Pharisee member of the Sanhedrin, he compared his lifting up on the cross for the healing of mankind with the lifting up of the brazen serpent by Moses for the healing of Israelites bitten by serpents (Numbers 21.8).

The effect, he said, would be that those who believed in him "should not perish but have eternal life." Given that he had just said that men were to enter into this new life "by water and the Holy Spirit," it is fascinating to hear him refer to the Cross as his baptism, a washing in his own blood (Matthew 20.22, Mark 10.38). James and John had asked for the highest places in his kingdom: he challenged them: "Can you drink the cup that I drink or be baptized with the baptism with which I am baptized?"

In the years before Cana, when he was a carpenter unknown outside Nazareth and not specially remarked inside it, did he know of the death he must die? Anyone can guess, but no one knows, for he does not tell us. We used to take for granted that the sword Simeon said would pierce through his mother's soul (Luke 2.35) "that thoughts out of many hearts may be revealed" meant the agonies her son's agonies would cause in her, so that she already knew. But Père Benoit sees it as the "Word of God"—*logos* in the Greek—which "is living and active and sharper than any two-edged sword, piercing to the division of soul and spirit, and discerning the thoughts and intentions of the heart" (Hebrews 4.12). Certainly it is hard to believe that the writer of Hebrews had not read Luke's second chapter.

What Jesus did know very early was the death men could die who called themselves Messiah. Judas of Gamala, one of three claimants who emerged when death had prised loose old Herod's grip, was a Galilean. The Romans left his body and two thousand bodies of his followers to rot on crosses at Sepphoris, a few miles from Nazareth. The small boy Jesus could hardly have gone outside his own village without seeing them.

One Roman official would succeed another, but with the same iron in the control and the same ferocity. Pontius Pilate, who was to send Jesus to his death, already had plenty of blood on the hands he washed of responsibility for the blood of Jesus—from Jesus himself we know of the Galileans whose blood Pilate had mingled with their sacrifices (Matthew 13.1). And Rome was to recall him from Palestine for a massacre of Samaritans.

So the two years of Christ's Public Life is not to be thought of as a Palestinian idyll, all sun-bathed, with the sick healed, storms stilled, Pharisees humiliated, sinners pardoned, crowds applauding. For him it was shadowed by the certainty of death at the end of the road.

But how black was the shadow? The words I have quoted about suffering to come are so very matter-of-fact, with not a hint of distress. What *did* it mean to him emotionally, spiritually? Did the certainty of resurrection take the anguish out of it? Did his divinity put him beyond the reach of anguish? Once only he speaks of the strain—"I have a baptism to be baptized with, and how I am constrained until it be accomplished" (Luke 12.50). He lived under a strain that never eased until it brought him near to collapse and death in Gethsemane.

Chapter IV

God or Man? Or Both?

I

There is a general idea that Christ's divinity was conferred on him by St. John! But there is nothing in the Fourth Gospel that goes beyond the "No one knows the Son but the Father and no one knows the Father but the Son" of Matthew 11 and Luke 10. John has Jesus speaking much more of Father and Holy Spirit, but our traditional formula "Father, Son and Holy Spirit" is not in John but in Matthew (28.19). It was before anything at all of the New Testament had been written that Peter called Jesus "the Author of life" (Acts 3.15). And before John's Gospel Paul had taken Jesus' divinity for granted with phrases like "God had sent forth his Son" (Galatians 4.4), and "In him dwells the fullness of deity bodily" (Colossians 2.9).

John is no cloudy idealist. His feet are very much on the ground. He likes detail. He alone gives us the marriage feast of Cana (2.1), the Samaritan woman with the five husbands (4.7), the blind man at the pool by the Sheepgate (5.2), the stink of Lazarus four days dead (11.39), Caiphas' highly practical reason for wanting Christ executed at once (11.48), the name of the man whose ear Peter cut off (18.20). John's account in chapter

44

9 of the man cured of blindness and his dialogue with the authorities verges on Dickens. And he punctures a lot of sentimentalizing about Judas with the flat statement "He was a thief" (12.6).

His conviction of Christ's divinity means no whittling down of the humanity. Rather he emphasizes it—possibly because he was writing after the Docetists had been teaching that Christ's body was not real and his death therefore not real either. He shows us Jesus at Lazarus' tomb weeping; in the days before Gethsemane begging his Father "Save me from this hour," on the Cross crying out "I thirst." That the death was real John conveys in half a dozen words: "Bowing his head, he gave up his spirit" (19.30).

Like all the Evangelists he sees and hears Christ acting and speaking on two levels—saying and doing things a man might, but also things that go beyond man's measure, and using the same "I" for both.

His "I thirst" on Calvary (12.28) is as human as the "My God, my God, why hast thou forsaken me?" that Matthew records (27.46). Countless men have known both those agonies. But "Before Abraham was made, I am" (8.59) claims pre-existence as no man can claim it; "I am the Bread of Life" (6.35) is farther still outside the human measure. "I cannot do anything on my own authority" (5.50) is an admission of the obedience he owes; so is "My Father is greater than I" (14.30). But "I and the Father are one" (10.30) is in the same category as those other mysterious sayings in which he applies one single measure to his Father and himself. We have seen his claim to an equality in inter-knowledge, each knowing the other as no one beside knows either (Matthew 11, Luke 10). John has more instances of this "bracketing"

—"He who has seen me has seen the Father—I am in the Father and the Father is in me" (14.9); "if a man love me ... my Father will love him, and we will come unto him and make our dwelling in him" (14.23). Observe how "No one comes to the Father but by me" (14.6) is balanced by "No one comes to me unless my Father draw him" (6.44).

So what were John and the rest to make of Jesus? They had to cope with a reality totally new in the world. There had been saviour gods in the myths, but they were so plainly mythical, their manhood as abstract as their godhead. In what century did Osiris flourish? In what town of what country did Mithra live? At what trade did Dionysus earn his living? But Jesus' manhood was real. He had for his first thirty years been so completely merged in the life of Nazareth in Galilee that it was the one place in which later "he could find no faith." After all, people there had known his father and mother, been to school with him, haggled with him over the price for making door-frames or ploughs.

It could not have been much easier for Peter and Andrew, James and John, fishermen on the lake—Jesus had his boyhood and early manhood in a town fifteen miles from that same lake and must have spent every spare moment in it or on it. Of his manhood they could be certain. And in a couple of years they had grown into the certainty that he was, however improbably, divine.

To begin with, there were the miracles, whole days filled with them, thirty-three described for us between Cana and Calvary. Eight show his power over inanimate nature; the rest are concerned with human beings —fifteen healings of diseases or bodily defects, a severed ear restored, two men and a girl brought back to life, six castings out of demons.

Even believers today find them an embarrassment. Yet flatly to deny that miracles happened would cause them a different sort of embarrassment, so interwoven are they with the whole Gospel story. So there is a tendency to take the line that they don't matter—which seems to me to be making the worst of both worlds: for what is embarrassing about the miracles is not their importance but their happening at all! I have several times been asked, "Does it really matter to you whether Christ fed five thousand with five loaves" (one per thousand, as a heckler once commented) "and some fish?" It matters indeed. If it did not happen, we are left with a wholly pointless bedtime story, which all four Evangelists thought worth telling. And, in any event, on the significance of this particular miracle we have a warning from Mark (6.51). When Jesus came walking on the water to the Apostles they were "utterly astounded, for they had *not understood about the loaves,* but their hearts were hardened"—Mark's way, or Peter's way, of saying that their minds were closed.

For a while, a reason for rejecting the miracles out of hand was the discovery at Epidaurus of limestone tablets, going back perhaps three hundred years before Christ, giving accounts of some sixty healings, credited to the gods Aesculapius or Apollo. The details are colorful—visits from the god in dreams, a woman five years pregnant, delivered at the shrine of a child who ran off at once to wash at a spring. But we do not know who wrote them, whose authority was behind them. In the myths there are plenty of such stories, but not on limestone tablets, not sixty all in one place. Were they meant for pious reading? Were they perhaps propaganda for the shrine?

Epidaurus is not much talked about now, the contrast in evidence between it and the Gospel miracles is too glaring. But why did Christ work them? What immediately occurs to us is that his power as a miracle worker probably saved him from being stoned to death for claims that must have sounded like blasphemy even to the poorest and least literate of his hearers. John gives a deeper reason. He always calls them signs— Jesus was calling on men not only to believe in his message, as the Baptist did, but in himself, as the Baptist did not. "The very works that I am doing bear witness that the Father has sent me" (John 5.36). Simply reading of the miracles gives us no notion of the effect upon those who saw them.

2

One advantage of reading—really reading—the Gospels is that we live through the years in which those closest to Jesus did not know what to make of him. We shall come closer to him ourselves as we follow their uncertainties. Their problems about him were real: that they came to certainty does not of itself answer those same problems for us.

They had no more idea than the crowd of what he was talking about when he made the eating of his flesh and drinking of his blood the condition of eternal life (John 6.54). It was too much for many of his hearers. But Peter could speak for the Apostles when he answered Jesus' question whether they, too, would leave him with "To whom shall we go? You have the words of eternal life." Thus early, Peter had uttered the essential Christian position, the foundation. Whoever Jesus was, whatever he said or did, they were sure of him.

The Twelve had been two years with him when he asked them who they thought he was. It is an astounding question: it means that in two years of close companionship he had not told them. It seems that he wanted them to grow towards the answer for themselves. Peter, again, answered, "You are the Christ, the Son of the living God" (Matthew 16.16). It was a milestone, but it was not the end of the road. Peter could hardly yet have seen as far as Thomas was to see when he met the risen Christ—"My Lord and my God" (John 20.28); as far as he himself was to see when he called Christ "the Author of life" (Acts 3.15); as far as John was to see when he wrote "The Word was God. . . . And the Word was made flesh and dwelt among us" (John 1.1–4). This too was a milestone, not the end of the road.

Christ was divine, Christ was human—two certainties. But how did those two realities meet in him? How could one "I" utter both? Where did one end and the other begin? What difference did the Godhead make to the manhood? Did it mean nothing to the Godhead thus to be living, functioning, in union with a man, this man?

These were questions for philosophers and theologians. The first Christian writers do not raise them. The Jews as a people were not given to philosophy. The Greeks were, but were of no immediate help: "to the Greeks," as Paul said, it was all "foolishness." Three centuries later Augustine could get no light from Greek philosophy on the problem of the Word made Flesh.

The distinction of person and nature, which has opened such a road into the mysteries of Trinity and Incarnation, the Greeks had not arrived at. Yet it was with tools furnished by Greek philosophy that Christian thinkers, of a dozen races whom the Greeks would have called "barbarians," were to construct a theology which Plato would surely have thought barbarous, utterly un-Greek. Among them we find Irenaeus (born somewhere in Asia Minor), Africans like Tertullian and Cyprian and Augustine, Egyptians like Clement and Origen and Athanasius, Italians like Ambrose and Leo I, Cappadocians like Basil and the two Gregorys, Syrians like Chrysostom and Ephrem.

But this lay in the future. As I say, the first Christians have left us no record of having asked our questions about what such a union between divinity and humanity might mean—not Peter certainly, but not John either, nor Paul. They drew world-changing conclusions from the union, but did not analyze it or try to "solve" it. They simply stated both elements.

Thus Peter could say that *"Christ was the Author of Life"*—and that he had died and been raised by God (Acts 3.15): Paul that Christ was *"the Son sent forth from the Father"*—and that he was born of a woman (Galatians 4.4). Even John, the theologian of the Twelve, simply set the two realities side by side. He opens his First Epistle: *"That which was from the beginning,* which we have heard, which we have seen with our eyes, which we have touched with our hands . . . *the eternal life which was with the Father* and was made manifest to us."

Christ *was* the only Son of the Father, but neither Christ himself nor John nor Paul ever discusses for us how a spirit can beget a son (though John, with his "Word that was *with* God and *was* God," opened the way to an answer). The Evangelists never ask what it meant that a God-man could be tempted. They simply recorded how men experienced the Christ who was God-man and who was tempted.

What I find most maddening about the New Testament is that it nowhere shows the Apostles talking among themselves about the Jesus they knew as no men on earth knew him. We listen in to no discussion of him among the Twelve, nor even between any two of them.

By the time of his Ascension they knew that he was human, the son of Mary; and they knew that he was divine, the Son of God. They must have wondered among themselves how the divinity in him accorded with things as normally human as his habit of praying to God, as heartbreakingly human as his "My God, my God, why hast thou forsaken me?"

Such questions they *must* have raised. But their writings do not raise them. These take for granted a Christ human and divine. On what the union of divinity and humanity in one person could mean they do not theorize. But if they shed no direct light on it, they drew a flood of light from it. To John and Paul, for instance, it was unique evidence of God's love for mankind.

"God so loved the world," says John (3.16), "that he gave his only Son, that whoever believes in him should have eternal life."

"He spared not his own Son," says Paul (Romans 8.32), "but gave him up for us all."

Dwell on these two. To Plato, four hundred years before, they would have been meaningless, as to Plotinus two hundred years after. The Old Testament was feeling towards them. They are at the heart of a new relation between the human race and God.

So the New Testament writers called on their readers to live in the fact of Incarnation as they themselves lived. The analysis could wait for the theologians. Here is Christ as men had experienced him.

When a man was to be chosen to fill the vacancy left by Judas, experience of Christ was stated as the essential qualification—he must be "one of those who have accompanied us during all the time that the Lord Jesus went in and out among us, beginning from the baptism of John until the day when he was taken up from us— one of these must become with us a witness to his resurrection" (Acts 1.21–22).

This experience was indispensable for apostleship: and for discipleship. We too must accompany the Twelve during all the time that the Lord Jesus went in and out among them. If Gospel reading is not that, it is not much. No study of theology is a substitute. We shall consider theology only after we have looked longer at the man God became.

In the Gospels we meet Christ, as the apostles did, mainly in his manhood. They saw him doing, heard him saying, things beyond the human measure. But that he who did them and said them was certainly human, they could not doubt—if only because they knew his mother! It was through his manhood that "the eternal life which was with the Father was made manifest."

And the work of our Redemption he performed wholly in his humanity. In Greek drama a god in human form would be lowered onto the stage by ropes to solve the insoluble problem. But God the Son actually became man, entering our race by way of conception and birth. In his manhood he suffered and died and rose again. There was no fiction anywhere in it. His divinity saved him no suffering. He knew the ultimate desolation of feeling nothing left to him but his tortured manhood, men's malice triumphant, God not coming to his aid.

I once met a Jew who had survived Hitler's Buchenwald: he had gone in confident in God, he came out with no faith in God left. God had forsaken him, he felt: there could be no God. For Christ the result was different: "Father, into your hands I commit my spirit."

Chapter V

To Save the Lost

I

When I was young in theology one of the burning questions was "Would Christ have come if Adam had not sinned?"

The liturgy seemed to answer with one of its best-known phrases, *O felix culpa*—"Fortunate the sin which merited for us so splendid a Redeemer." This sounds like saying that if the race had not "earned" Christ by sin, it would have had to do without him. Put less crudely, it meant that if the first Adam had not sinned there would have been no need for the second. For this view the great authority quoted was the Dominican, Thomas Aquinas. But his younger contemporary, the Franciscan Duns Scotus, held that the Son of God would have become man in any event, in order to crown the union of the human race with God which was the whole point of creation.

It is not so long since Dominicans and Franciscans were at each other's throats about it, teeth bared. But by the time I had reached my theological middle age the debate had drained away into silence. The Scotus view was taken for granted by theologians generally, by me certainly. I had forgotten the whole matter until I found myself censured by a reviewer for not clearly casting in my lot with Scotus!

How remote it all seems. Adam and his sin, for instance: nobody would go to the stake now, or send anybody else to the stake, over the precise meaning of the Genesis account of man's beginnings. Who today would speculate on what would have happened if Eve had eaten the forbidden fruit and Adam had not? Or if Adam had and Eve had not? Certainly the Gospels do not tell us; Jesus never directly refers to Adam at all.

Whether God the Son would have become man if man had not sinned is a profound question in its own right. As I say, the general view of the experts is that he would. The world's sinfulness did not cause the Incarnation, only affected the manner of it. But to the ordinary Christian the question seems almost hopelessly academic, at best an unreal option: men *have* sinned, and who can imagine men sinless?

The immediate question for us is anyhow not how Christ would have acted in a different world, but Why did he come to this one? Several times he tells us what he came for. Consider the reason he gave for staying in the house of Zacchaeus, a rich tax collector, loathed therefore by his fellow Jews: "The Son of Man came to seek and to save the lost" (Luke 19.10). He certainly brought about a marvellous change of heart in Zacchaeus—"Behold, Lord, the half of my goods I give to the poor; and if I have defrauded anyone of anything, I give it back fourfold."

Of the half-dozen explanations Christ gives of his coming, I have begun with this one, for two reasons. First, all the other "I came" statements—such as "to bear witness to the truth," and "that men may have life and have it more abundantly"—are related to it. Second, it links with his name, Jesus, which means "Yahweh saves," and with the reason given to Joseph for the choice of the name—"because he will save his people from their sins." He came as saviour and redeemer, and what especially he came to save the world from was sin.

If emphasis on sin now strikes people as morbid, the emphasis—and the morbidity?—are definitely Christ's. "I came not to call the righteous," he says, "but sinners" (Matthew 9.13). I have seen a document, issued by a Catholic society, on the teaching of morality: it urges us not to talk about sin, because the only sin Christ objected to was legalism, that is, taking the commandments seriously. In fact he names a number of sins which cannot be written off like that.

Glance at the line-up of sins which he says "defile a man," that is make him filthy: "evil thoughts, murder, adultery, fornication, theft, false witness, slander" (Matthew 15.19). The sin for which it would be better to cast oneself into the sea with a millstone round one's neck was not legalism but causing his "little ones" to commit sin. To the men whose paralysis he healed—in Capharnaum (Mark 2) and at the Sheep Gate in Jerusalem (John 5)—he said "Go and sin no more": he was not warning them that they must not be so legalistic in future. They were just plain sinners like you and me. The healing at Capharnaum is unique—the only miracle worked to prove a particular point, and the point was that he had "power on earth to forgive sins."

But as things now are, "saviour" touches no welcoming chord, "sin" no chord of regret. The life has oozed out of both words. And where does that leave Jesus?

When we hear Christ say that he has "come to seek

and to save the lost" (Luke 19.10) we take for granted that
he is talking of sinners. Why? A man is lost when he is
off the right road and does not know how to get back on
it. Lostness is at its dreary peak when a man does not
even know he is off it and naturally makes no effort to
get back. This is the ignorance that is bliss. While it
lasts.

Sin, then, is only one way of being lost, lostness cov-
ers a larger area; and in all that area Christ is saviour.
Yet it is a right instinct that makes us think instantly of
sinners when he speaks of the lost. In the immediate
context that is what Christ meant, for he was explaining, to a crowd shocked by it, his friendship with a swin-
dling tax collector. And in the context of his whole life
there is nothing to compare in urgency with his will to
save sinners. If we are seriously to face the problem of
showing our world—and ourselves, perhaps—what difference Jesus might make, we must think long upon the
present standing of the words "saviour" and "sin."

For the present "saviour" need not detain us. In the
sense in which Christians have used it for nineteen centuries it has almost vanished from the language. One
hardly ever hears it, even from the pulpit. Who believes
in eternal damnation? Hell is for the birds, they say
elegantly. Hell went into the discard earlier than
heaven. For vast numbers of believers both words survive only in jesting phrases—like heaven for climate,
hell for company. Heaven is not longed for, hell is not
feared.

What about sin? I remember a snippet of conversation I came across in a short story—" 'People used to call
it sin,' she said with a giggle." That giggle you can hear
everywhere. Sin as a breaking of God's law means less

and less, or rather has meaning for fewer and fewer people, mostly middle-aged or old. "What harm," we are asked, "do our so-called sins do to God?"

Actions which damage others are of course wrong. That is the one test our world is agreed upon. But there is no limit to our skill in sidestepping the test when our own interests are involved. Taking away a wife or husband, for instance, usually hurts the one left behind, but . . . she has been making his life a hell (or he hers, as the case may be) for years; or the woman's nerves are shot to pieces by not having him (her psychiatrist is definitely alarmed for her), *or* it would be so much better for the children; *or* surely we are civilized people. . . . In no time at all conscience is assuring the one who wants the break that it would be highly immoral not to do the thing they are lusting to do. Conscience is having a new lease of life as an ally of desire.

An even stronger instance of the test being sidestepped is abortion. Killing a baby in the womb most certainly damages it, whether it is small enough to be drawn out by suction or large enough to need its skull crushed first. Killing a human being which has done no wrong is precisely the definition of murder, yet for this particular slaying of the innocent any reason apparently will do.

"A woman has a right to do what she likes with her own body": but the foetus is not part of her body, it has its own chromosomes and genes, different from hers. "It is not yet a human being": one medical man calls it "garbage": but human it certainly is: if it is allowed to live, it cannot grow on into anything but a man or woman. "It may be killed as an unjust aggressor is killed in war": but it is not an aggressor at all, it did not put itself there, the parents did.

A woman might decide that in the special circumstances her well-being is of more value than the child's life: at least she should realize what it is that she is doing. But in the slaying of a foetus as in the taking of another woman's husband, as in the slaying of hundreds of thousands of Japanese in a couple of flashes, in the killing of civilians by all armies in all wars, one particular wheel has come full circle. The teaching that the end justifies the means used to be charged against the Jesuits as the high point of their villainy. Now it is accepted as a common-sense rule of conduct.

So Christ as saviour of the lost will get no great hearing in our world, if we think of "lost" as meaning only sin-stained. But, to repeat, that is only one way of being off the right road. There is a here-and-now lostness, one which not only will nobody deny, but which to thinking men everywhere is a torment. And for this too Christ has the remedies.

2

It sounds like a rather pointless truism to say that for community there must be unity, but in a breakdown truisms come into their own.

There is a community when the members have the same scale of values and standards of conduct, the same goals and the same priorities, general agreement as to things desirable and things intolerable. Mentally they are living in the same world, have the same view of how things ought to be.

The view may be inadequate, but provided it is taken for granted there is community. It may have in it elements which to men of a different view would be wholly unacceptable—like the homosexual structure of Sparta; slavery in Greek democracy; the ancestral spirits feared by the Australian aboriginal; the one-time exposure of girl babies in China to death by freezing; eunuchs as priests where the Earth Mother was worshipped. These things may work for the destruction of a community from within, but no one of them makes community impossible if people in general find it acceptable.

In a community long established, homogeneous, ways of life exist, taken for granted, not seriously questioned. They are livable, men feel at home in them. But if too large a number cease to feel at home in them, and find them in fact unlivable, then community is fractured: all over the structure appear cracks and fissures which must be mended or they will bring down the whole. This is now happening rather notably here.

We are in a time of crisis, a Greek word for judgment, and our judgment is going to be fearfully tested. Rule of thumb will not serve, when thumbs point every way. We can no longer play it by ear, when every man's ear is tormented by a different jangle of tunes. There is no agreement on the changes needed, no agreement on what's wrong, one man's healing would be another's wounding. The mind must go to the imperilled roots. It is long since our societies took their roots seriously, so enjoyable were the fruits. Even for the root-men—that is what "radical" means—roots are only to be pulled up, that we may start again rootless.

In America the Constitution still stands, but the country is already a different country. The Founding Fathers would not recognize it as their own; neither would Lincoln, nor Theodore Roosevelt. Franklin Roosevelt would have taken it for granted. He had seen the beginning of values and moral standards which in a quarter of a century was to become the norm, the vanishing of any line clear to everybody dividing the desirable from the intolerable.

What happened between the two Roosevelts? Two world wars and such a surge of technological mastery of the material universe as had never been known. But the confusion in the mind had already begun. Till the middle of the nineteenth century the moral principles accepted in the West on personal and political life were still recognizably Christian. They were not always acted upon, but they were not denied. There was a lot of façade about it, but not only façade. The tyrant and the rebel equally felt bound to show how Christ would have approved their actions. The public conscience demanded it. Then came Marx to eat away old certainties, and after him Freud, and after him Einstein. Even where, as in America and England, the structures still stand, there is a different humanity inside them. And the challenges our way of life has received are as nothing to those which await it, from the drug craving at one end to the computer at the other. And waiting in the wings there is the test-tube baby, whose mother and father have never met.

What *is* the root? Community should at least be in agreement upon, and base its values and priorities upon, what man is and what life is all about—why man is here, what comes next, whether anything comes next. This test our liberal democracies cannot pass. Any citizen may, according to his religion or philosophy, hold that man is a union of matter and spirit, or that he is matter only but evolved, or that he is spirit only, and that at death he may or may not perish totally.

But the State as such is neutral, it simply does not know: it is controlling men's lives more and more, but regards the nature of man and the purpose of human life as no affair of its. But not to know why man is here or where he is supposed to be going is precisely to be lost. In that lostness Christ could come to our aid. If we want aid.

In the writings of advanced thinkers I keep meeting the Contemporary Man—he has, among other things, "recognized his commitment to the world." In real life I rarely meet the man they describe. When I do he nearly always turns out to be a writer himself. Yet whole philosophies and psychologies are being modernized to allow for what he insists upon in religion and what he will no longer accept.

Albert Camus, to take an example, says that he has "a nostalgia for totality, a longing of the heart for clarity." I once brought this into a lecture. My hearers stolidly wrote it in their notebooks. I went on to say that the man thus described was not a type familiar to me— "Yourselves, for instance. If you have a nostalgia for totality, a heart that longs for clarity, I can only say you conceal both remarkably well." They wrote that too, with unruffled stolidity.

My own generalizations about today's average man are on a less lofty, less literary, level. The key to them is that he not only doesn't know, he doesn't even wonder, why the universe—himself included—is here, where (if anywhere) he is to go next, how he is to get there (if there is any there). That man I meet everywhere, at my lectures often enough, brought by his wife.

But, as we have noted, not to know why, or where from, or where to, is to be lost. And Christ came to save the lost. So why don't we just move in and give him Christ?

The difficulty is that he doesn't know he is lost. He

has no "nostalgia" for the right road, no "longing of the heart" to know where he is—it never occurs to him that he doesn't! With this, as with so many of the needs that only Christ can meet, the need has to be brought to awareness in men. They are tormented by a whole tangle of urges and appetites, some good, some base. But only at odd moments are they troubled by the mind's profounder needs, as for hope or purpose or meaning in life. As a result futility is the very air they breathe, and the indulgence of the body's appetites is futility's inevitable resource. But of the body's appetites they are continually aware, of the mind's only occasionally.

Occasionally? The frequency varies from person to person, so does the depth of the gloom. One feels almost physically the what-the-hellness of everything—the meaninglessness of life in general and one's own individual pointlessness, one's lostness in a universe growing larger by the minute, one's helplessness under the presence of forces mankind cannot control or measure.

It rarely happens, I think, that such moods turn our average man's thoughts to Jesus of Nazareth. *He simply does not relate to men's felt needs.*

One reason, I think, must be sought in the picture they have of him, the bits and pieces of the Gospel Jesus still lying about in their memory. The one thing universally remembered is his kindness, in support of it are Bethlehem cribs at Christmas time, a handful of hymn lines. Pause for an instant on Charles Wesley's

> Gentle Jesus, meek and mild,
> Look upon a little child;
> Pity my simplicity. . . .

Gentle, meek and mild—those adjectives do not add up to a man you would want in a crisis. You remind me that they were to be sung by a little child. But even little children seem to be different now, I don't know any who would want to sing about their "simplicity." Even in the tinies, simplicity runs neck and neck with cynicism about their elders; and how early marijuana moves in.

The association with childhood is a real barrier between Jesus and our world in fracture. One does not automatically think of him as a masculine male. The sense of something less than manhood is aided by statues all liquid with love; and many of the paintings of Jesus by Old Masters give the impression that the artist used a female model.

There is one mood to which the gentle Jesus appeals, not always healthily—I mean the remorse which accompanies the satiation inseparable from too much feeding of bodily appetites. One hears it said, for instance, that Christ was too kind to want us to suffer the pain involved in keeping some of the Commandments. I knew a man, not a Catholic, who in his convalescences after too much sinning sought out Catholic churches for the peace he felt in them. He probably knew Edward Eickersteth's line "The blood of Jesus whispers peace within." We must look more closely at Jesus to see if he was kindness and nothing else, whether the peace he promised was as simple as this.

He did mention a sword.

Chapter VI

The Pharisees

I shall not keep repeating, but we should never forget the heavy strain under which Jesus lived his public life. "How I am constrained," we have heard him say. He lived in the awareness of what awaited him—baptism in his own blood at the hands of men he had come to save, hatred from men for love of whom he was dying. We have seen the strain in his calling Peter "Satan" (Matthew 16.18) for urging on him the very thing he himself was to ask his Father in Gethsemane. And that is not the only time we see—or think we see—its effects on moods and words and actions.

It accounts, perhaps, for the occasional impatience. "Have you no sense, no wits, are your hearts dulled? Can't your eyes see, can't your ears hear, don't you remember . . .?" (Mark 8.17, Knox Version). This was said not to high priests and scribes but to his chosen Twelve: he had warned them against the leaven of the Pharisees and of Herod, and they thought he was talking about bakers' bread.

Something of the strain he actually utters with "Faithless and perverse generation, *how long must I bear with you?*"—this again not to his sworn enemies but to the Apostles and the crowd, after the Apostles had failed to exorcise a demon.

With the first public miracle he had moved out of the cover of the carpenter's shop into No Man's Land, which the world he entered was (and our world has become). It has been a habit of preachers to lavish all their energies upon the torments of a Roman flogging and a Roman crucifixion in order to wring compassion from the congregation—which after all knows that Jesus rose again and ascended into heaven. The real value of knowing just what the horrors were is that we can measure the resolution with which he continued the attacks upon the Establishment which ensured their happening. He could know impatience, he could know shrinking of the heart, but he never deviated.

I

The picture of Jesus, gentle and meek and mild, would have surprised High Priests, money-changers, Pontius Pilate, Peter and the rest of the Twelve. It would have stunned the Pharisees, the scribes especially. Listen to some of the items in the long catalogue of their faults we find in Matthew 23:

"You serpents, you brood of vipers, how are you to escape being sentenced to to hell?" "Woe to you, scribes and Pharisees, hypocrites! For you are like whitewashed tombs, which outwardly appear beautiful, but within they are full of dead men's bones and all uncleanness." "You travel sea and land to make a single proselyte, and you make him twice as much a child of hell as yourself." "They bind heavy burdens hard to bear, and lay them on men's shoulders, but they themselves will not stir a finger to lift them." A little earlier we read, "The tax collectors and harlots go into the kingdom of God before you" (Matthew 21.31).

He accuses the scribes of hypocrisy, "They do all their deeds to be seen by men"; of greed, "They devour widows' houses and for a pretense make long prayers" (Luke 20.46). Hypocrisy and greed are of course to be found in all religions, including our own. Why did Jesus concentrate on the worst? Why, above all, did he not seek personal contact with the best? Not with the Sadducees perhaps—they had the Temple and the majority in the Sanhedrin, Judaism's governing body: they knew how to handle the Roman conquerers—Annas had got the High Priesthood out of them for himself and in succession for his five sons and a son-in-law. But the future was not theirs. With the destruction of City and Temple they vanish from history.

Israel's future was with the Pharisees, who survived and have wonderfully preserved the faith of Israel through all the centuries since. Clearly they were going through a bad period, but there were splendid men among them. There was Gamaliel, at whose feet Paul boasted that he had sat; Joseph of Arimathea, who provided the tomb in which the dead Christ was laid; Nicodemus, who provided the aloes and myrrh for the linen shroud, and who had dared to speak a word for Jesus in the Sanhedrin, a mild enough word, but it took vast courage. We are told of Jesus' meeting with only one of them, Nicodemus (he "came secretly, by night, for fear of the Jews"); but there is no suggestion that Jesus criticized Israel to him or discussed it at all: the conversation was wholly about the New Birth needed for entry into the kingdom of God, a new idea, not found in the Old Testament, and the key to Christ's understanding of his mission. There must have been contacts of which the Gospels do not tell—Joseph of Arimathea had become a disciple, and Pharisees were among those who joined the Church after Pentecost. But the main line of Christ's ministry by-passed them. We may wonder why he made so little effort to win the most vital element in his own people.

After all, such men would have agreed with him totally about the faults he attacked—the great rabbis attacked them as he did. But his real criticism of Israel went to the very depth of Israel's religion as scribes and Pharisees generally had come to see it.

Read the account of his healing of a withered hand (Mark 3.1-6). It is the first time we are told of his showing emotion—and the emotion is anger. "He looked around at them with anger, grieved at their hardness of heart." Pause a moment upon this combination of anger and grief. As I wrote in *To Know Christ Jesus,* it is "a reminder that he was like us, not only in possessing a human nature but in his way of being human. We too can be angry with those we love, while grieving at the failure in them which roused our anger: and who knows whether the anger is greater or the grief?"

What matters for our present enquiry is that his anger was not at bad scribes and bad Pharisees. Even the best of them might have thought that healing was forbidden on the Sabbath. For many a Jew the Sabbath rest *was* Judaism. It was taught that they might carry nothing heavier than a fig, there were extremists who held that the prohibition of work extended to bowels and bladder.

"The Pharisees went out and immediately held counsel with the Herodians against him, to destroy him." The Herodians were not a religious party, their aims were political—to restore Herod the Great's kingdom to his son Herod Antipas. To quote from my same book, "Not for the last time religious idealists and tough politicians worked together for tragedy."

We must look more closely at the reason why such as Gamaliel did not accept Jesus.

When the Sanhedrin, predominantly Sadducee, "were enraged and wanted to kill" Peter and the Apostles (Acts 5.33), Gamaliel, most famous of Pharisees, urged: "Let them alone; for if their undertaking is of men, it will fail; but if it is of God, you will not be able to overthrow them. You might even be found opposing God."

It is a wonderful saying. And we are back at the question what might have happened had Jesus opened his mind to Gamaliel. Perhaps part of the answer lies in the next sentence: "So they took his advice, scourged them and let them go"—an odd way of "letting them alone." And soon after we have Saul "breathing threats and murder against the disciples, dragging off men and women to prison." The Establishment was too strongly entrenched. The conversion of Nicodemus and Joseph of Arimathea did not cause a ripple. Would even Gamaliel's? And would he in any event have been converted? As we grasp the complexity of the Pharisaic system and its hold upon every detail of daily life, we marvel that any of them left it for the new way.

For Christ's message was wholly revolutionary, putting the axe, not to the roots certainly, but to a great part of the tree—a tree whose fruit they had found good, in whose shade they had adored God's majesty. They were not philosophically minded: what life God might have within himself they seem not to have asked, but only what he did for men and required of them. Saul, become Paul, was to say of them, "That they are zealous for God's honor I can testify, but it is with imperfect understanding" (Romans 10.2).

The Old Testament tells of God's love for men as clearly as the New, comparing it with the love of a father (Psalms 67.6, 102.15), even to the love of a mother (Isaiah 49.15), which the New does not. But for the Pharisees, Majesty was the word: majesty is easier than love to handle legally: their whole emphasis was on man's duty to obey his commands.

These were found in the Torah essentially, the five books of Moses, but also in the Prophets and the Holy Writings which make up the Old Testament. As conditions changed, the laws had to be applied to new situations. This was the world of the scribes. Where the Christian theologian has God himself as the prime object of his theologizing, the Jewish scribe had to devote all his mind's energies to God's laws for men. The general result was what Catholic theology might have been if produced only by Canon Lawyers.

The laws of the Torah were analyzed more and more minutely, to meet every conceivable situation. There were the great basic matters of Sabbath observance, Temple and sacrifices, circumcision; rituals, ceremonials, were prescribed with a precision which grew incredibly. There were washings after contact with some things, before contact with others, foods that could not be eaten, ritually unclean people with whom one must not eat, whose houses one must not enter. (Glance at Mark's chapter 7.)

Only the strictest Pharisees observed all the hundreds of precepts, but there was general observance. And there was nobility in it, with self-mastery learned, and discipline grown habitual. Yet at best there was a danger, external observance rated too high, the essence missed. And at its lowest, there could be a twisting of the precepts to serve self-interest. "How do you say 'we are wise and the law of the Lord is with us'? Indeed the lying pen of the scribes has wrought falsehood." This is not Jesus speaking, but Jeremiah six centuries earlier. (8.8)

When Jesus said, "You leave the commandment of God and hold fast the tradition of men" (Mark 7.8), he is commenting on the accusation made against the scribes by Isaiah (29.13)—"In vain do they worship me, teaching as doctrines the precepts of men."

Through all this tangle Jesus cut a swathe. *Washings?* What's the point of making clean the outside of the cup, it's what the cup contains that matters: inside the scribes he found "extortion and rapacity" (Matthew 23.25). *Food?* "What goes into the mouth does not defile" (Mark 7.15). "Thus," says Mark, or Peter rather, "he declared all foods clean." The *Sabbath?* It is made for man, not man for it. The *Temple?* Not a stone of it will be left standing: but that is not the point—"God is a spirit and must be worshipped in spirit and in truth." With stroke after stroke he cut away beliefs and practices which had come to seem the very essence of religion.

With the ablest of the Pharisees he might have discussed many of these points, profitably, lengthily. But there were matters of difference weightier than these, and his time was short. He went direct to the people.

2

So Christ took his message direct to the people, by-passing not only their rulers but their religious leaders as well—the Sadducees who held the High Priesthood and the Temple where alone sacrifice could be offered, the Pharisees whose influence was strong in the synagogues to be found in every town and village of Judea and Galilee. The main point of his message was of the New Order he was founding of a re-born humanity. Along with that had necessarily to go criticism of the order then in possession.

In that order there was hypocrisy in plenty, and Christ attacked it again and again. But the best of the scribes and Pharisees were not hypocrites—not Nicodemus or Joseph of Arimathea who accepted Christ, or Gamaliel who did not. Rigid external observance did not mean hypocrisy—one remembers Rabbi Aqiba who, a century after Christ, supported Bar Cochbar in his claim to be Messiah and in the rebellion which the Romans crushed with their usual horrible efficiency. The small ration of water allowed by his Roman captors he used for the ritual washing of his hands before drinking the drop that was left. He welcomed his execution as a fulfilment of the command to love the Lord his God with his whole heart.

But rigid external observances—eatings, washings and the rest—could become an end in themselves and, as such, a distortion of reality. The word "sinner" often enough meant one who had defiled himself by the things he ate or the ritual washings he neglected. In teaching explicitly that nothing that goes into a man's stomach can defile him but only what comes out of his heart (Matthew 15.10–20), Jesus was overturning a vast structure of religion held by some of the best of his race. Yet in the overturning he could quote Isaiah: "This people honors me with their lips, but their heart is far from me" (29.13).

It is the heart—or, as we should now say, the will— that is decisive. Christ's call was for repentance—the Greek word *metanoia* is best translated "change of heart." Just as nothing a man eats can defile him, nothing a man does can damn him—only if he loves himself to the exclusion of God and his fellow men.

The word "exclusion" reminds one of a second element in Pharisaism. I wrote in my book *To Know Christ Jesus:* "There was another danger, not inescapable, but not easy to escape either. Israel was unique among peoples, the Pharisees were unique in Israel. Only heroic humility can bear uniqueness; and in any religion heroic humility is likely to be the virtue of a minority." There is a danger of exclusivism, and arrogance is its shadow. There existed a real contempt for the mass of Jews, the illiterate, lumped together as the People of the Land, "the accursed multitude which knows not the law": it mattered less if such as these believed in Jesus (John 7.49). And in too many Pharisees a failure to grasp the true nature of Israel's uniqueness led to a belief that whatever the kingdom of God might prove to be, it would be theirs, with the mass of mankind secondary to them.

The primacy of spirit and the equality of all men in God's sight were not the only or the greatest things in the life Christ brought: but they made the only atmosphere in which the life could be lived.

One result of Christ's all-out attack on scribes and Pharisees is that it provided a detailed warning to the

Church he was founding. He warned his followers that scandals would certainly come: and the scandals, which have in fact come so copiously through the centuries, are marvellously like the evils he listed in his own Israel. In the fourth century St. John Chrysostom could say: "We imitate the hypocrites, we even surpass them." There is no century in which that could not have been said.

Was Jesus, then, consciously and intentionally warning his own followers? Once at least he seems to be: "And in the hearing of *all the people* he said to *his disciples* 'Beware of the scribes' " (Luke 20.45). One might have expected a statement of attacks by the scribes on the young Church. But what we get is a list of scribal defects: so that the danger of which his followers must beware is imitation, yielding to the same human weaknesses: "They like to go about in long robes, and love salutations in the market place and the best seats in the synagogues and places of honor at feasts"— all harmless vanity, you think; but Jesus continues: "They devour widows' houses and for a pretence make long prayers: they shall receive the greater damnation."

So greed for money is the damnable element—then, now. We shall have to look closely at what Christ has to say about money.

Chapter VII

Values and Priorities

The thread on which the chapters of this book are strung is the question, What difference does Jesus make? The answer springs instantly to Christian minds. The difference, effective eternally, lies in his work as Revealer and Redeemer.

As Revealer he laid open to us the innermost life of God and the innermost meaning of man, so that we may live in the full light of reality instead of in the half-dark, knowing what we are, why we are here, what comes next, knowing our goal and its splendor and how we are to reach it.

As Redeemer he bridges the gulf sin had made between mankind and God, establishing a oneness between men and God in Christ which lifts life to a new level here and brings man to maturity hereafter: in that maturity all human energies will be functioning at their highest in relation to God and one another, so that we are at last fully men and not the rough sketches of humanity which is all that even the best of us are here below.

So far I have hardly touched on all this. I have not spoken of either the revealing or the redeeming, but only of the one who revealed and redeemed, into whose life we are re-born, in union with whom we are to reach fullness of life and abide eternally in it. I have two reasons for this.

First, the deeper level calls for Faith. It lies beyond our gaze, there is no evidence for it but his word. The Christ we meet in the Gospels is the ground on which Faith stands.

Second, the Realities revealed are of a magnitude, and what I may call a texture, beyond our habit. Mind and heart need strength to carry them.

> Human kind
> Cannot bear very much reality,

says T. S. Eliot in *Ash Wednesday*. But they make the world in which Christ lived mentally, and as we grow in intimacy with him we can become citizens of his world, increasingly at home in it.

So he must be studied as one of ourselves, literally a brother, not dehumanized by the divine in him or taking illicit advantage of it to by-pass life's sufferings, but tempted as we are in all things, coping with the life we must cope with.

He establishes the standards and values by which the pleasures and pains, the privileges and duties, of life on earth must be judged: by that alone the difference he makes, to men who have such uncertain standards and values, is immeasurable. And only as the Man Christ Jesus becomes ours shall we begin to live in the mightier realities, especially Redemption, especially the part we are called upon to play in it. For a while longer we shall stay on this first level, seeing what we can learn from him about life and death, love and law, sex and marriage, freedom and morality, money, the Jewish religious Establishment and our own—in general, his priorities in the matter of human relations, which is where most of man's joys and pains are.

I

Which human vice does Jesus attack most often? One thinks instantly of hypocrisy. But it seems to me that he rates love of money as worse. After all, he did not scourge hypocrites. And nothing we actually hear him say to them equals what he says of wealth: "You cannot serve God and money"—this is in the Sermon on the Mount (Matthew 6.24) and again at the end of the Parable of the Unjust Steward (Luke 16.13). And his comment when the rich young man went away was: "It is easier for a camel to go through the eye of a needle than for a rich man to enter the kingdom of God" (Matthew 19.24).

One has heard efforts to scale down the starkness of this by noting that a very narrow gate in the wall of Jerusalem was called the needle's eye: one wonders why, having thus enlarged the aperture, they don't diminish the camel, finding perhaps, that "camel" was a Chaldean word for donkey. Jesus meant to choose the sheerest impossibility—the largest animal at work in Palestine, the smallest aperture. Hence his further comment: "To men it is impossible, but to God all things are possible"—even the salvation of the rich. It is a matter of common observation that the rich do not possess money, money possesses them: even when they want to use their wealth well, the amount of time and energy they have to give to holding on to it, to say nothing of increasing it, occupies their mind to the neglect of the mind's higher functions. Christ says: "The cares of the world and delight in riches choke the word so that it

proves unfruitful" (Matthew 13.22), that is, wealth steril-
izes. "They are stifled by the cares, riches, pleasures of
life and never reach maturity" (Luke 8.14).

And what is maturity? Seeing, living, life as a whole,
not solely the fragment of life here on earth between
womb and tomb. Refusing to decide between two brothers arguing about an inheritance, Jesus warns against
covetousness, wanting more than our needs, and tells
the parable of the Rich Fool (Luke 13.13–21). This man is
saying to himself: "Soul, you have ample goods laid up
for many years . . . take your ease, eat, drink, be merry."
But God said to him "Fool! This night your soul is required of you. And the things you have prepared, whose
will they be?" Ponder the parable. And ponder the next
thirteen verses, comparing our notion of our needs with
Christ's notion.

Nothing is clearer in his teaching than the transi-
ence of our life on earth—it is a road, not a dwelling
place. We have duties, to love and serve men here, to
develop the earth God made for us, and our life will be
judged success or failure according as we perform
them. But the end is not here. "I go to prepare a place
for you," he says (John 14.2). "If hand or foot or eye lead
you into sin, cut off hand or foot, pluck out eye: it is
better for you to enter life with one of each than to be
cast into hell with two" (Matthew 18.8).

The earthly things we treasure may be valuable or
worthless, either way they will pass. "Lay up to yourselves treasures in heaven. For where your treasure is
there is your heart." And the heart is decisive. How is
the rich man to lay up treasures in heaven?—for the
rich man can be saved, thanks to God's omnipotence.
Normally by using his money for good. That is surely

the meaning of the parable of the Unjust Steward. His employer had discovered that he had been cheating him and demanded to see the account books. The steward could not do anything with the accounts—the auditors were already in, so to speak. Out of a job, with no future, he decided to win the friendship of some of the debtors by using the money he still had to pay off part of their debts. As he used his money to win him earthly friends, let us use ours to win the friendship of God.

But for perfection, Jesus told the rich young man, "Sell all you have, give to the poor, follow me."

It is possible that in these repeated warnings of the dangers of wealth, Jesus had deeply in mind the Church he was founding. Had ecclesiastics observed them more closely, there would not have been the great breakaway at the Reformation. One remembers that the money-raising crusade for the building of St. Peter's detonated Luther: that in Henry VIII's first attacks on the Pope, Parliament was wholly with him because of resentment at Rome's continual draining of money out of England: that the monasteries Henry seized were largely in the hands of money-lenders because of the building mania of their Abbots.

And the first sin we find punished in the new Church (Acts 5) was the lie Ananias and Sapphira told about money. We may feel their punishment excessive, but when we realize the harm money has done to the Church. . . . Churchmen, of all people, should be afraid to look a needle in the eye.

2

When Jesus said, "You cannot serve God and money," his Pharisee hearers "scoffed at him"—they were money-lovers themselves, says Luke (16.14). In reply Jesus stated the basic fact about his own values and priorities: "What is highly esteemed among men is an abomination in the sight of God." We dare not simply take that in our stride: he is talking about love of money, but the possibility touches everything.

The reason for the contrast in values is that we let this life fill our whole horizon as it did not fill Christ's —and does not fill reality's. Even those who believe there is another life find that it does not exert the same ceaseless pressure on senses and appetites as this life exerts. But this life is only the first stage; slowly or quickly it must pass; the next stage abides without end. That is the point of the parable of Dives and Lazarus, and the parable of the Rich Fool who was complacent in his financial invulnerability—but his soul was required of him that night!

All this may seem to invite the materialist parody,

> Work all day, feed on hay—
> You'll get pie in the sky when you die.

But the parody is a parody. In this place or that, Rich Christian Fools may have used Christ's emphasis on the next world as a reason why people should put up with exploitation in this. But the whole effect of him has been quite other. Proletarian rebellions, for instance, have been a commonplace within Christendom, scarcely known outside. In social-political progress— the abolition of slavery for instance, the rights of the individual, the rights of women and children—the world that has known Christ is far ahead of the world that has not.

For Christ's steady assertion that the next life matters more includes no suggestion that this life and our handling of it do not matter vastly. He teaches clearly that the self which will enter the next life is the self which by decision and action we are forming here on earth. What we *do* now decides what we shall *be* after death. How can it devaluate our actions here to say that they have everlasting consequences?

So Christ gives us principles and guidelines for our handling of ourselves and our relations with others: as sociology they have never been surpassed. The idea, for example, so long basic to our laws, that every man is of value and has rights, simply for being a man, reaches us wholly from him. That his principles have never been fully lived up to is a weakness in men, not in them. They have been part of the making of the world the Christian has lived in. They still condition his responses, so that in acting against them he is aware of doing violence to something in himself—and this even when he hardly remembers that they are Christ's, even when he does not advert to Christ at all.

Christ's principles, I say (and hardly need to say), have never been lived up to fully. There is a weakness in the will, which shrinks from the efforts and self-denials that his way calls for. And this is interwoven with a weakness in the intellect which has never concentrated on discovering the meaning in depth of what he is saying. As to the will's weakness, Christ must continuously provide the Life which will strengthen us—we shall discuss this later. But for the intellect's we remind ourselves that Christ, who is the Truth, has already provided us with all that we need.

It may at first strike us as strange that the clearest

reason he gives against our acting as if we rated this life above the next is that it is foolish. Immediately after his promise to Peter of the Keys of his Kingdom (Mark 7.21), we find him giving a catalogue of things flowing out of an evil heart which "defile a man." He names twelve of them, based on the Ten Commandments. Five of these are *actions,* involving our fellow humans—adulteries, fornications, murders, thefts, slanders; six are *states of mind*—evil thoughts, coveting, malice, deceit, lasciviousness, envy. It is a frightening list—if few are guilty of all, few are guilty of none. It culminates in pride, the choosing of self against God. And Christ can summarize the whole list by its twelfth item—foolishness!

It sounds like an anticlimax. To rate the transient above the everlasting, to rate self above God, is indeed foolish. But does foolishness defile, is it an abomination? There is indeed a silly foolishness which does no great harm. But there is a gross foolishness which really does make men gross. Fornication, for instance, is talked of today by religious men and women as harmless, enriching even. Robert Burns, who knew more about it than most, says:

> It hardens all the heart
> And petrifies the feeling.

Christ has made a selection of the ways of indulging impulses and appetites which flow from the folly of rating this life above the next, grabbing the immediate pleasure or profit and damning the consequences. The evil of all of them is the damage they do to the "heart." Saint Augustine answers splendidly those who argue that, because the body doesn't matter, sins in the body don't matter either. The body will indeed return to the dust, but its sins will live on in their effect on the self. What Burns has said of fornication is true of them all, they harden the heart, make it harder to penetrate, close it to any interest that conflicts with self-interest.

That this is what really matters about any misuse of ourselves explains a curious fact about the Parables—those, I mean, which are concerned not with the kingdom but with the individual human being; you, for instance, and me. They all treat of sin, but have not much to say about sins: they contain nothing like the catalogue of sins in Mark 7. There is a man who showed no mercy though mercy had been shown him, one who beat his fellow servants and went on drinking parties, one who wasted his employer's goods, one who lived riotously. There are no murders mentioned, no slanders, no sexual sins—though riotous living and drinking parties presumably did not exclude such. The main concern in these parables is not the great sinner but the average man—talents wasted, God's gifts unused, the self indulged, emptiness, futility. In any given parable the point is not the particular sin, but only the state of heart from which sins proceed.

Jesus is not writing out a prescription. He is not prescribing a pill but a way of life, not something we take but something we become. He wants our health—health of heart, health of soul. Either word means the whole self, just as the Scripture phrases "my spirit," "my flesh" are simply ways of saying "I," as the *Et cum spiritu tuo* of the Latin Mass means "and with you." Indeed the New English Bible substitutes "self" for "soul"—"What shall it profit a man to gain the whole world and lose his own self?" (Mark 8.36).

What is the self's health? To be like God, perfect as

Christ's heavenly Father is perfect (Matthew 5.48). We are made in God's image, the image is marred or mutilated by sin, our whole effort must be to work with Christ for its restoration. As Jude puts it, "God yearns jealously over the spirit he has made to dwell in us" (4.5). That, of course, is not Jesus' phrase: it is Jude's translation of John's phrase "God is love," and John's phrase is the distilling of all that he learnt from Jesus about God and man. It is a uniqueness of Christ's teaching that he makes love the whole point. Out of the six hundred precepts the scribes drew from the Torah, he selects two phrases from Deuteronomy—"Love God with all your mind, heart, soul, strength" (one's whole "self," in fact), "Love your neighbor as yourself" (the self that loves God, of course). Upon them he makes the Law and the Prophets, commands and teachings, depend. They are not a substitute for these, but their life principle.

Jesus does not define love, he shows it in action; he does not often speak of it as feeling, almost always as doing. There is our love for himself, for instance: "He that has my commands and keeps them, he it is that loves me" (John 14.21). There is the love we must show other men: we must bear one another's burdens, we must bear *with* one another—in other words, we must give and forgive. There is no limit to the giving—the greatest love man can show is to lay down his life for his friend (John 15.13). There is no limit to the forgiving: unto seventy times seven.

How does this apply to the love God wants us to have for Himself? Our experience of loving either things or people does not seem to apply readily to loving God. Yet it is one same love, at two stages of growth: "If we don't love our brother whom we see, how shall we love God whom we don't?" (1 John 4.20).

3

No text stirs people from the pious coma in which, as we have so often noted, most people read Scripture, as much as Jesus' saying in the Sermon on the Mount that a man who follows a woman with his eyes, lusting for her, "has already committed adultery with her in his heart." Their instant reaction is to feel that there is a world of difference between revelling in the thought of adultery and actually committing it: the lady, not to mention her husband, would certainly see a difference.

But Jesus has a way of concentrating on one element in a situation at a time, balancing other elements later. Here he is thinking only of the effect of lust on the man who gives himself to it, the effect on the heart. The same distinction is made in the Decalogue, where adultery and coveting are the object of separate commandments, as are stealing and coveting. What a man makes of the self he begins with, this is Christ's continuing concern: upon that, actions good or bad are not decisive, only the condition of the heart which produces them and is strengthened or defiled by them.

This is why prayer matters—a conversation between the self which is ours and the self which is God's. Call it self or heart or will, union between ours and God's is the goal of our life as it was of Christ's. "He learnt obedience by the things he suffered" (Hebrews 5.8). So must we. "Jesus offered up prayers and supplications with loud cries and tears, and he was heard for his godly fear" (Hebrews 5.7). With "fear and trembling," says Paul, "we must work out our salvation" (Philippians 2.12).

What lies in the way of the union between the self and God? The self, of course. To be sinless, says the grimly ironic Augustine, we have only to will it. Only to will it. . . . So many other things attract the will calling for no effort save to let go, calling above all for no surrender of autonomy.

When parents tell their children that they must learn self-control, they think of self-control as control of one's words and actions, holding back from doing thus and thus. In this indeed we all make some sort of progress, or life in society would be impossible. But self-control means control of the self itself, silencing the clamor of self-interest, and the craving for self-assertion. And how much progress have any of us, parents or children, made in that? To measure our progress we have the Sermon on the Mount (Matthew, chapters 5 to 7), which is a sermon especially on love of God and love of neighbor, more profoundly on the self and its control.

We must be poor in spirit, which means that we must see ourselves life-size: humility comes from *humus,* "earth," which we barely rise above. We must be patient —the world does not revolve around us, is not geared to our requirements. I am not entitled to special treatment for no better reason than that I am I. Aquinas puts it perfectly: "When everyone seeks his rights, there is chaos."

We must be pure in heart, willing not what we want but what God wants. To our coming into existence and to our remaining in existence we have contributed nothing. Sin is an effort to add pleasure to existence against the will of God which alone holds us in existence. In that sense sin is suicidal. Awareness of this does not, unfortunately, prevent us from sinning, but it makes us feel fools all the same, and that is a beginning of wisdom.

On the border between the Sermon's treatment of our handling of ourselves and our dealings with others, comes "If a man hits you on one cheek, offer him the other." It is often quoted as against killing, in war especially; but it is only against resentment of insult. A smack on the face may hurt one's dignity, but it is not lethal. Self-importance is what Christ the psychiatrist, doctor of the psyche, is here trying to correct.

Our dealings with others, he sums up in the Golden Rule (Matthew 7.12): "Treat others as you would want them to treat you." Here (as elsewhere) we find him making obvious applications—"Bear one another's burdens," "Feed the hungry, clothe the naked," "show mercy," "forgive wrongs done you" and a dozen more. In the Sermon he points out how we can break the Golden Rule, hardly aware that we are breaking it.

Observe that Jesus is not offering for our approval a literary or philosophical essay on ideal human relations. He is deadly serious—half a dozen times in the course of the Sermon he sounds the warning bell—salvation and eternal loss are at issue.

The sheer foolishness of our treatment of other people runs like a thread through the Sermon on the Mount. A clear instance is in our way of judging their actions, motives and characters as if either we ourselves were sinless or at least our sins were mere trifles in comparison with theirs. Just indignation is a two-edged sword: I know a man who cannot get the pleasure most of us get from indignation at the sins of ecclesiastics, because to think of anyone else's sins always reminds him of his own. To his credit be it said that he never spoils the party by mentioning this.

But with judging others as with so much else in the Sermon, the foolishness is not the main point. If we judge others we are inviting God to judge us, says Christ Our Lord (Matthew 7.1), and there is always something fearful about judgment on his lips. As I have said, he is in deadly earnest. He is not telling us that it is nice to be nice, kind to be kind. Niceness, kindness, are a long way from "hunger and thirst after righteousness." Throughout the Sermon he warns that eternal happiness or eternal loss depend on our decisions.

Two points are worth noting here. The first is that Jesus speaks always as though our own choices are to make the difference: from end to end of the Gospels there is not a hint that anyone is predestined either to heaven or hell. We cannot be saved without Christ's redemptive action certainly, but we cannot be saved unless we co-coperate with Christ or damned unless we refuse him.

The second is that while he gives us two commandments—"Love God, love your neighbor"—on which all the rest depend, we rarely hear him speak of eternal loss resulting from failure in what we owe God, almost always from failure in what we owe our neighbor. In chapters 3 and 4 of his First Epistle, John shows us why. "Whoever does not love his brother is not of God. . . . If anyone has the world's goods and sees his brother in need, yet closes his heart against him, how does God's love abide in him? . . . If anyone says 'I love God' and hates his brother, he is a liar; for he who does not love his brother whom he has seen, cannot love God whom he has not seen."

Elsewhere we have noted everlasting fire as the destiny of those who do not feed the hungry, clothe the naked, visit prisoners and the sick (Matthew 25). In the Sermon on the Mount we have: "If you do not forgive, your heavenly Father will not forgive you" (Matthew 6.15). The man who is angry with his brother beyond limit "shall be liable to hell fire" (Matthew 5.22). We have noted how following a woman with one's eyes lustfully is adultery in the heart. Jesus continues "If your right eye causes you to sin, pluck it out and throw it away: it is better that you lose one of your members than that your whole body be thrown into hell" (Matthew 5.30).

The condemnation of the man to whom mercy had been shown and who proceeded to treat another man mercilessly is to be that of everyone who "does not forgive his brother with all his heart" (Matthew 18.35). And Jesus has a special warning to anyone who leads others into sin: "It would be better for him to have a great millstone fastened round his neck and to be drowned in the sea" (Matthew 18.6, Luke 17.2).

Jesus constantly stresses doing the will of God. He has it in the Lord's Prayer; those who do it are his "brother and sister and mother" (Mark 3.35); he utters his own total acceptance in the worst moment of his agony (Mark 14.36). There are some who will be excluded from the kingdom of heaven, though they have prophesied in his name, even worked miracles in his name. Why? They have not done his Father's will. But almost every *example* he gives is of failure to live up to

God's will *that we should love our neighbor*. And as the highest point of man's loving, Christ gives not love of God but that he lay down his life for his friend (John 15.13). Eternal failure is a refusal of love. If self has been the god one has chosen to serve to the exclusion of the love of neighbor and therefore of God, then self is what one is left with at death, God and neighbor alike excluded.

Yet God will not give up any man lightly. Christ tells us that we must forgive one who does us wrong unto seventy times seven (Matthew 18.22)—provided of course that he is sorry, as Luke, treating the same episode, points out (Luke 17.4). There is still more love, more forgivingness, in God. How many sins, one wonders, were forgiven the notorious sinner in Capharnaum because she loved much (Luke 7.47)? And the thief on Calvary had left his repentance very late to whom Jesus said, "This day you will be with me in paradise."

4

Jesus has a way of speaking which is not ours. Indeed it is sometimes so different from ours that we can miss the point of what he is saying.

This comes mainly from his being a first-century Jew, his Galilean friends would not have had our difficulties (in Judea the Galilean accent might well have exposed him to a certain mockery, as did Augustine's African accent when he was speaking Latin in Italy). His ways of speech were Jewish. There were certain words very much his own, notably Abba, Father—it was not the Jewish habit to address God so intimately; and Amen—a word used as an emphatic introduction only by him in the New Testament. But in general he used Jewish idioms and thought-forms to say things no Jew had ever said, utter thoughts those thought-forms had never contained.

There was the whole Scriptural way with numbers, using them not as arithmetic but as rhetoric—the figures really were figures of speech. Forgiving unto seventy times seven was a way of saying we must never refuse forgiveness if the offender is sorry—it would need a very industrious offender to offend against us 490 times (or seven times in a day, as Luke has it). So it is with "more joy in heaven" over one sinner repenting than over ninety-nine good men with nothing much to repent. So also with the shepherd leaving the ninety-nine sheep to go and look for one that was lost—no shepherd would take that literally, and in human flocks lost sheep are more than one in a hundred. The numbers were to emphasize the vast importance, in the first case of forgiving, in the second of repenting, in the third of never giving up on a sinner.

Overstatement as a device to force attention applies not only to numbers. To those who heard him say them the words "many are called but few chosen" (Matthew 22.14) would have meant only that not all who are called are chosen. It was a way of stating not the rarity but the difficulty of salvation. So was "the gate is narrow and the way hard that leads to life, and those who find it are few" (Matthew 7.13)—one's own salvation must not be taken for granted. There have been modern Christians brought near despair by taking both sayings literally.

Consider two other examples. Jesus says that some "make themselves eunuchs for the kingdom of God" (Matthew 19.12): that superb thinker Origen took the words literally and carried them out. Later he realized that they were no more than a way of saying, unforgettably, that one may be called on to serve God's kingdom by celibacy.

There could hardly be a more startling example than "If anyone does not hate his own father and mother, wife and children, brothers and sisters, yes even his own life, he cannot be my disciple" (Luke 14.26). Hate sounds strange as a condition of being disciple of the one who made all the Law and the Prophets depend on the two commands of love. One remembers the brothers Andrew and Simon, James and John, among the Twelve, the love of Lazarus and his sisters for each other and of Jesus for all three. But his Jewish hearers knew that "hate" need be no more than a colorful way of saying "love less." In Matthew (10.37) we find it translated accordingly: "If you love father or mother more than me, you are not worthy of me." And in Matthew the context is provided. The effect, not of course the purpose, of Jesus' coming would be "not peace but a sword," a deep cleavage between those who accept and those who refuse. Members of the same family will be ranged on one side of the cleavage or the other. The disciple will be on Jesus' side, whoever may be on the other.

With this we are back at his values and priorities. The top priority is to do the work of God. To the man who said "Lord, let me first go and bury my father" (Matthew 8.21), his answer was "Follow me, and leave the dead to bury their own dead." It sounds harsh, it is harsh. But it is a choice that may have to be made, because of the immensity of the issues involved. We see them fitfully, Jesus saw them steadily, lived in the awareness of them. Love cannot serve men better than by doing the will of the God who is love.

Life is not a game, with prizes for the winners, consolation prizes for the losers. "Every tree that does not bear good fruit shall be cut down and cast into the fire" (Matthew 7.19). Interpret "fire" as you will, you cannot make it into a consolation prize. It is sheer desolation. Jesus is a doctor healing diseases in the self itself—it would be no kindness in a doctor not to tell us what the diseases are and what their consequences.

Chapter VIII

The Gospels and Ourselves

I

So far we have touched lightly on Jesus as Revealer and Redeemer. We have been studying the Jesus who revealed and redeemed, as we meet him in the Gospels—his character and what we should call his personality. His message draws its power to win men, not primarily from its own splendor but from being his. It is worth our while to have a midway pause for reflection on the Gospels.

As I have said, I do not mean the bits and pieces still left when the most destructive critic has done his worst. I mean Matthew, Mark, Luke and John, as men have seen Christ in them through nineteen hundred years. The critics have a vast amount to teach us, but only if we already have our own personal knowledge of him. Otherwise they can only dazzle and daze us.

This is specially true of those who hold that Jesus was simply a Galilean carpenter with some special insights, whom some of his followers "worked up" into the Jesus of the Gospels. So far this has not much concerned us, because it does not cause its holders to question the general picture we have found in the Gospels of the kind of person Jesus of Nazareth was. Some of those who are most convinced that John is the worst offender in putting words into Jesus' mouth admit that on the ground level, so to speak, there is a quite special actuality and factuality about John—on the humanness of Jesus, for instance, and on the details of life in the Israel which had been swept away twenty years before his Gospel appeared.

But with Revelation and Redemption, to which we are now coming, we leave ground level, and the scholars will be making their criticisms felt. These we shall consider as they arise. Here I would like to make one general comment on the whole theory of a Church-invented Christ. All the "inventing" it assumes must have been carried out at extraordinary speed. Christ was crucified about the year 30. The first three Gospels are usually placed (roughly) between 60 and 80. That would not leave very much time for so very much invention. And most of the Epistles are earlier. In 1 Thessalonians—not much more than twenty years from Calvary, Paul himself a Christian only fifteen years —we find Father and Lord and Holy Spirit, Christ's redeeming death, his resurrection and our own, the Second Coming. In 1 Corinthians, written about 58, Paul tells of having taught Christ's resurrection and ours on a visit six or seven years earlier still, tells too of the establishment of the Eucharist and Christ's reality in it. Before 60 comes the theological masterpiece Paul wrote to the Romans—whom he had never visited.

If so much doctrine—utterly new and of a profundity which has held and enriched minds ever since—was invented at such racing speed, one wonders who invented it. Not the Apostles, surely. The tongue-tied group around Christ show no genius save a genius for not understanding him. The Sanhedrin saw them (Acts 4.13) as "uneducated common men"—"illiterate nobodies" would translate the Greek words. Why should the teaching that the Gospels attribute to Christ not have been his? It seems almost wanton to write off as its author the one genius we actually know about, and imagine anonymous geniuses who within thirty years of his death produced so amazing a body of teaching and persuaded new Churches so widely scattered to accept it.

The Gospels (as Luke tells us about his own) were not written as a first introduction to Christianity, a Beginners' Course. They were written, as were the Epistles, to people who had already received a basic instruction. What this contained is nowhere stated, the writers assume it as known. What we do know is who was in control of it. Paul tells the Galatians how he checked with "those in repute" in Jerusalem on the Gospel he was preaching, lest he should be "running in vain," and how with their endorsement (he mentions James the Less and Peter and John) he and Barnabas went forth to the Gentiles. That their control was strong and effective we know—Paul (dead thirty-five years after Christ) could write to Churches he had never visited, certain that what he wrote would be in harmony with what they had been taught. The experience of Easter and Pentecost, to say nothing of what happened after, meant that they would see meaning in many of Christ's teachings which they had seen only dimly when they heard them. They would find new wording and phrasing. But invent? One would need stronger proof than I have seen yet.

2

We are moving from the kind of man Jesus was to the teaching he gave. And whereas, among those who really know the Gospels, there is a pretty general agreement about the man, the disagreement about the teaching is fantastic. It has flowered over the centuries into hundreds of different churches bearing his name, and though ecumenism raised hopes of widening agreement, the difficulties in the way of it look all but insoluble. Yet we must try to solve them, or at least to understand them. The differences are of such quality and quantity that whoever is right, great numbers must be wrong—which means that they are not getting what their Redeemer wants them to have. Since they all take the Gospels as basic, clearly the disagreements must arise either from the nature of the *Gospels* or from the *minds* men bring to their reading. It would be folly to enbark on a closer study of what Jesus taught without an examination of both these elements, in which better men than we have missed their way through the ages.

We begin with the second. As a first step, consider the mental atmosphere of the world we inhabit—its ideas and its assumptions, its values, intellectual and moral, its discoveries and what it makes of them, its vocabulary. We all have to live in this atmosphere; we cannot help breathing it. In what I have to say of it I shall be using some phrases from the lengthier treatment in Chapter 2 of my *God and the Human Mind.*

Every age has its mental atmosphere. The decisive element in ours is its total secularity, the assumption that what we can experience—through our senses and the instruments which extend the senses' range—is the limit, not of the possible precisely, but definitely of man's concern. God is not actually denied, He is not considered at all. Life is to be conducted without reference to Him. Secular ethic, for instance, means deciding on rules of right conduct *as if* God did not exist, without settling whether He does or does not. For the mind of our time God is a question that simply does not arise. He is hidden in a cloud not of His own too much light, but of man's unconcern.

In this atmosphere we have no choice but to live. There is a continuous seeping in from it which makes for a kind of damping and discoloration even of things we would die rather than deny. We may not accept its denials or its doubts; but we are most certainly affected by its emphases.

This is a peril even if we are strongly grounded in the Faith: to those who are not, the peril is enormous. They may perhaps have given little mind to what Christ actually taught. Being loyal Catholics, they have accepted what their teachers taught them without questioning, that is without penetration, thereby reducing all virtues to the virtue of obedience. But when Christ gives a revelation, he is telling us something, not just testing our capacity to swallow. A mere willingness to believe whatever God says—"Certainly, dear Lord, if you say so" —is a poor skeleton of the virtue of obedience, and no skeleton at all of the virtue of Faith. It means that from the truths themselves they receive no nourishment, and indeed expect none. The connection between doctrine and nourishment has escaped their attention.

Meanwhile our world—so brilliant technologically, so innocently sure that in it mankind has at last come of age—dismisses the whole religious "thing" as of no importance. A Christian can feel embarrassed at the difference between his own beliefs and its cool certainties. There is great psychological value in a strong affirmation, said Hilaire Belloc. No affirmation is stronger than our world makes of its own maturity: a Christian can all too easily find that such affirmations as he is able to make cannot match its strength. There comes a kind of scaling down and shading off, a switching of the mind away from beliefs at which the people he meets would raise an eyebrow. His instinct is to try to get into step with everybody else, while not actually abandoning truths grown insipid. This instinct is especially strong today. But it was there at the very beginning of the Church. St. Paul warned the first Christians against it: "Be not conformed to this world, but be re-formed in the newness of your mind" (Romans 12.2).

There comes a point beyond which we must be out of step with our generation. If our following of Christ is a reality and not just a gesture, we hear a music that others do not hear. It sounds for us in the Gospels, provided we have not let it be drowned out by the clamors of our world.

In considering the minds we bring to the reading of the Gospels, we have glanced at the effect on them of the mental atmosphere of the world in which we live our daily lives. The books, for instance, that we ordinarily read, the periodicals, the newspapers—it would be a mockery to ask if the ears attuned to them are likely to catch all the music of the Gospel message.

In today's mind no place is left for the supernatural, whether seen as God's intervention in man's life here, or as manhood's coming to its fullness in union with God hereafter. But these are what the Gospels are about.

Throughout the ages initiation into divine mysteries has been the main point of religion: the Gospels are aglow with it. In the mental air we all breathe today there is not an echo to be caught of it. "Love the Lord thy God," which Jesus makes the First Commandment, strikes the typical modern ear as merely quaint. On the other hand, love for our fellow men, which Jesus places second to it, receives full honor, not strictly as love, perhaps, at least as an admitted duty of service to others. Men who give no thought to God can work against cruelty and injustice with a devotion which makes the efforts of too many believers seem pallid. But our admiration for such men can easily become part of that "seeping in" of which I have spoken; we hear Catholics, too, speaking of the service of men here on earth as if it were the whole of religion, as if life here on earth were all that matters, with God and the hereafter left aside. To men of this mind the Gospel Christ is not attractive.

> I am sure this Jesus will not do,
> Either for Englishman or Jew.

Blake might have been writing of our own day.

But quite apart from "the infection of the world's slow stain," there is the person each one of us is. We have our own individual minds, characters, temperaments, obliquities, stupidities, obstinacies, and these can operate against a full reception of what the Gospels are there to give us.

There are things in them which this or that reader finds it hard to swallow—the Virgin Birth, or angels (especially bad ones), or future events foretold, or the dead raised to life. There are things some find morally revolting—"Depart from me ye cursed into the everlasting fire," "Whose sins you shall forgive they are forgiven," "If you love father or mother more than me, you are not worthy of me."

From all such difficulties there are two ways of escape, the way of the plain man and the way of the scholar. The plain man simply switches off his attention. He reads them as if they were not there: people can read the Sermon on the Mount, for instance, without noticing that it mentions hell five times. The way of the scholar is different. He does not—not always anyhow—ignore texts he cannot accept. He simply weighs them on a separate scale. Texts that suit him he accepts without inquiry, texts that don't are subjected to microscopic scrutiny. A single text is all he needs if it says what he wants said: whereas two are dismissed if they don't. Thus we are told that the Virgin Birth is only in Matthew and Luke—only! We are reminded that Luke *alone* gives Christ's visible Ascension (he is the only Evangelist scientifically trained, and he gives it both in his Gospel and in the Acts). We shall be noticing other examples of the double standard as we come to them. I mention it here as a warning to all of us.

We have considered, sketchily it must be admitted, the mind that is brought to the reading of the Gospels. A tougher problem is the mind that is not brought. There are many who could not care less what follows this life, who are as exclusively concentrated on the here-and-now as any cow on the patch of grass under her nose. There are people who seem to be God-deaf, as others are tone-deaf, there are God-blind people as there are color-blind. Listening to God is as meaningless to the one sort of deafness as listening to music to the other. How we are to bring them to Gospel reading I don't know—the music-lover and the tone-deaf cannot communicate.

Back to ourselves. If we are to make the universe of revelation our own and live at ease in it, we must use the mental muscles—for gripping spiritual reality and absorbing it—which the daily run of life seldom calls for. Otherwise we may be accepting revelation as true, without feeling it as real. Under the pressure of temptation, we may find ourselves wondering whether it is there at all. The answer is in Christ. As he grows real to us, the universe takes on some of his reality. His certainties become ours.

3

Differences among Christians about what their Teacher taught arise from differences in the mind each reader brings to the reading of the New Testament. They arise even more inevitably from reading it as what it is not. Too many simply do not realize that all of it was written for people who had already received a basic instruction in the Faith: for that basic instruction it is not a substitute; it is supplementary to it. It does not set out the instruction for us, simply takes it as known.

The men who wrote its twenty-seven books would have been astonished to find it treated as if it were final, inclusive, exclusive, so that "nothing need be believed which is not clearly contained in it" (to quote two leaders of another Church). Indeed they would have been surprised to find it called "it"—they did not know they were contributing to a book. They would have been still more surprised at hearing it called the "New Testament." For the New Testament shows no awareness of its own inspiration, or indeed of its own existence. Apart from Luke's reference to his own Gospel at the beginning of Acts, only one of its books mentions any other, namely 2 Peter—which itself got into the New Testament by the skin of its teeth, when the Church was making its definitive selections and rejections. It mentions, without naming, some writings of Paul's, not to tell of their inspiration, but to warn that "the ignorant and unstable twist them to their own destruction" (3.16). And that is the whole of the New Testament's reference to itself.

As I wrote in *God and the Human Mind*, "By the end of the first century the New Testament was complete, the last Apostle was dead. It was the end of an age, the age of personal contact with the Christ of this earth. Men do not seem to have felt it so. We are not to imagine them counting the Apostles, as one after another they died, saying at last 'There's only John left,' and at his death breathing an almost desperate 'Thank God we have their writings.'"

In fact it was another half century before the books of the New Testament secured their place as a definite element in Christian life—to be read at Mass on Sundays, for instance, along with the Prophets. By the year 200 the New Testament was accepted by the whole Church as canonical, its contents established very much as we now have them (one test for inclusion being conformity with a pre-existing body of doctrine). To those early Christians the Church was the teacher—if the New Testament is not mentioned in the New Testament, the Church is on every page of it. There is nothing said in it even about the Old Testament to compare with Paul's calling the Church "the pillar and the ground of truth" (1 Timothy 3.15). The Apostles' Creed, based on one used in Rome round 160, goes straight from "the Holy Spirit" to "the Holy Catholic Church."

All these first writers assumed that their readers had already been instructed in the Faith. Some indeed say it in so many words—like Paul writing to the Thessalonians and reminding them of what he himself had already taught them "either by word of mouth or by letter." Luke opens his Gospel by telling Theophilus that he is writing it "in order that you may understand in all its certainty the instruction you have already received."

What then was—is—the New Testament's special contribution? Paul's Epistles, for instance. We have some dozen of them, written over a period of fifteen years. The Jerusalem Bible reminds us that they are "occasional writings, not theological treatises, but responses to concrete situations." He writes of elements in the doctrines which had been misunderstood or contradicted, of false ideas or ill practices arising in one place or another: he will suddenly, to our delight, introduce ideas on which his own mind had been working towards new clarifications.

He does not mention any particular fact or doctrine unless something in the situation calls for it. If his first letter to the Corinthians had been lost, critics would have asserted that he "knew nothing of" the Eucharist as Christ's body and blood. You would rub your eyes to see what they have made of his not referring to Christ's Public Life. In fact he had no occasion to: the errors he was writing to correct did not involve it—that would come later with the Docetists, the answering of whom accounts for so much that is exciting in John's Gospel.

The Epistles deal with "concrete situations," with Christ's revelation as men responded so very variously to it. They may be compared with the Church's official teaching as medical case books with a medical textbook. In medicine both are essential. In Christianity both are priceless.

4

In the last half century there has been a subtle shift in the centuries-old discussion of the Christ of Faith as contrasted with the Christ of History. As things are now, both are the inventions of scholars. The Christ of History is still what they think they can establish about the Carpenter of Nazareth by approved historical tests. (What they thus establish tends to vary between nothing at all and nothing worth having.) But whereas the Christ of Faith used to be the one whom believers found in the Gospels, he is now as much of the Gospel Christ as the scholar himself finds spiritually relevant—an essence of Gospel distilled by each scholar for himself as all that really matters. Between the two Christs who emerge from so much learned exploration, the Gospels are a shambles.

"The early Christians," writes one, "did not distinguish between history and myth"—history meaning what in fact took place, myth meaning such elements in the Gospel story as the writer himself cannot accept but is prepared to find all the truer for not having happened. The miracles, the foretelling of the Crucifixion, the Resurrection, the teachings on Trinity and Word-made-flesh, heaven and hell—these are myth not history. The Christian community, it is said, stimulated by its conviction that Christ had risen from the dead, produced them between the death of Christ and the writing down of the story. In this theory what the Gospels give is the Christ that the first Christian community had come to believe in: it is for us to accept him through faith in these our ancestors, having first sorted out from their ideas what is spiritually profitable and intellectually credible to ourselves.

But in the four Gospels we have not merely the Christ in whom the second-generation Church believed but the Christ whom his Church knew from the beginning. The Evangelists were not writing history but recording living experience, their own or that of men known to them. The second-generation Christians believed in the Christ that the first-generation Christians had known. Learned men brush aside too easily the unparalleled power the Gospel Christ has exercised over the souls of men in every time and place. Anyone who can read the Gospels and not feel the power in them simply cannot read.

There was no such gap as the development and spread of myth demands. Christ died round the year 30. Writing about him had come early. Luke, writing about 60, tells us of "many *before him,*" who had "undertaken to compile a narrative of the things which have been accomplished among us, just as they were delivered to us by those who from the beginning were *eye-witnesses* and ministers of the word." Mark and Matthew we know of: but Luke's "many" must mean more than these two. And years before Luke, Paul was writing to the Corinthians reminding them of the teaching on the Resurrection he had given them seven years earlier still, twenty years from Christ's death.

As to the creative community, one can only wonder

which community they have in mind. Mark's Gospel (which was largely Peter's) was written in Rome, Matthew's in Palestine, John's in Ephesus, Luke's in Caesarea or wherever Paul's journeying or captivity took him. All four were accepted at their face value in every part of the Church, their veracity not questioned save by men who broke away, as Marcion did. Clement of Rome, writing in the 90s, quotes passages from the first three. Ignatius of Antioch, who barely survived the end of the first century, brings John's Gospel into his letters. After that quotations become a flood. Irenaeus, writing in Gaul, just after the middle of the second century, quotes the New Testament eighteen hundred times. Origen in Egypt a century later about eighteen thousand.

The Christian community as the *source* of the Christ of the Gospels seems to me as wholly an invention of scholars as the Christ of Faith and the Christ of History. Whenever in the New Testament we come across Christian groups scattered over an area a couple of thousand miles long, we find them receiving instruction, not imparting it. In that sense there was no concrete Christian community, but a highly concrete teaching authority. Yet we can get a kind of composite photograph of the Christian community from Paul's Epistles. Those first Christians are quite horribly like ourselves, and about as creative.

The Gospels are four portrait studies of Jesus of Nazareth as he was known to men among whom he lived and died. Like the Epistles they were written not as a first introduction, but to be read by people who had received a basic instruction in the new religion. Each of the writers could have said of his Gospel what Luke said at the beginning of his: "It has seemed good to me to write . . . that you may know the truth concerning the things of which you have been informed." And each of them could have said of his Gospel what John said at the end of his—"Many other things Jesus did which are not written in this book." So that when Gospel A mentions some word or deed which is not in Gospel B, it is foolish to assume that Evangelist B did not know it. When so much is admittedly omitted, it is unsafe to build an argument on particular silences.

All four move to the climax of Christ's death and resurrection—one quarter of their total treats of the single week between Palm Sunday and Easter Sunday. Clearly that had to be the main point of any report on the Redeemer. But both as to the happenings of that week and as to what went before, each made his own selection according to the purpose he had in writing.

Christ died round the year 30. The first three Gospels go back to the 60s, roughly the same interval as between the Second World War and now: the things they relate happened in a country no larger than Vermont or Maryland: great numbers of those who knew Christ there would still have been alive. They are called Synoptics because composed in one general shape and using a good deal of the same material, which must have already existed in the Church. But it was not a matter of a top copy and two carbons.

Matthew had been the tax collector Levi to whom Jesus said "Follow me." His theme is the kingdom (he uses the word over fifty times) considered especially as the fulfilment of God's plan for the Israel of the Old Testament. From Papias of Hierapolis, who died in 130, we learn that he wrote for Jewish Christians in their own language. This Aramaic version we no longer have. What we have is a Greek version made, scholars think, after Mark but before Luke, with the addition of some of the same matter as we find in one or other of them.

According to the same Papias, who had known St. John, and to Clement of Alexandria who came a generation too late for that, *Mark* wrote down what he had heard Peter preach—about Jesus' life and work, but most richly of his personality. It is, as the others are not, what we call a human document: no one of them so vividly conveys what it meant to live through the Jesus years, taking the shock of each new incredibility as it happened. I find it natural to read "I" or "me" whenever Peter's name occurs in this Gospel. Which does not of course prove anything!

Luke, Paul's "beloved physician" and frequent companion, was the only Gentile among the four, a Syrian. It seems clear that he conceived his Gospel and the Acts of the Apostles as one continuous treatment of his master theme, the universality of the kingdom—not the Chosen People only, nor, among the Gentiles, only an elite: he quotes Isaiah, *"All flesh* shall see the salvation of God." As Matthew shows the kingdom growing *from* Israel, Luke shows it growing *into* all humanity. He is more of a historian than the others, but modern historians are uncomfortable with him because of his continuous awareness of the action of the Holy Spirit. "Spirit" is Luke's key word as "kingdom" is Matthew's.

It is usually held that the Fourth Gospel was written in Ephesus in the 90s; there is a question as to whether it was written by St. John or by a disciple of his (or by a different man of the same name, otherwise unknown). What John's purpose was he tells us clearly—"these things are written that you may believe that Jesus is the Christ, the Son of God, and that believing you may have life in his name." He is writing a full generation, thirty years or so, after the others. All that had happened in that period—within the Christian body, in the world outside, and in his own soul—had shown him what elements in Christ and his work most needed emphasis. In the phrase quoted he shows these as three above all— the *humanity* of Jesus (which Docetists were calling a fiction), his *divinity* (which Cerinthus was denying), and the *life* into which men must be reborn.

There we have our four portraits. They are from different angles, the lighting is different, the brushwork different. But each is by one who, to apply Wordsworth's test, "kept his eye on the object." With all their individuality, they are all portraying the same person. Of them as a whole, we may say what a critic has said of Luke's account of Jesus' first appearance among the Eleven after his resurrection—they are "a warning to us not to sever the original Christ from the tangible Jesus."

Chapter IX

The Universe of Jesus

"The universe of Jesus" is one of those phrases—"life of Christ" is another—which would have a different bearing now. To us "life of Christ" suggest a biography, but throughout the New Testament it means the life he came to bring us. "Jesus' universe" might suggest that we are about to ask whether his "all nations" included the Antipodes and how much he knew of modern astronomy. But our concern is with the structure of the reality in which he mentally lived, and in which we too must live mentally if we are to have the mind of Christ.

I

There is God, there are men, there are animals, there is the world of matter. All this we take for granted about him, there is nothing in it to shock our modernity. But he believed in angels. (For what it is worth, I note that apart from one quotation from Isaiah, the New Testament angels have no wings.) There are those who think he was only humoring his Jewish hearers: they believed in angels (the Sadducees didn't): it was a harmless belief, so he brought angels in. But with what conceivable object? Try as I may, I cannot write out this theory without making it sound idiotic.

111

He was not much given to humoring his hearers. He had come into the world to give testimony to the truth, and this involved the uprooting of so much that they valued—ritual laws, Temple, Sabbath, the reverence due to scribes and Pharisees. In any event he brings angels in as no Jew ever had. The "little ones"—children, the uneducated—had angels "who see the face of my heavenly Father continually" (Matthew 18.10).

Vivid in the Jewish mind was the word of God to Moses (Exodus 33.20): "You cannot see my face, for man shall not see me and live." And for the Israelites Moses was greater than the angels. It is true that in the non-Scriptural book of Henoch four angels are spoken of as "angels of the face" because they stand before the face of God, but there is no hint that they gaze on the divine face. In the century after Jesus the greatest of all Jewish rabbis, Aqiba, said that the angels who "carry the throne of glory do not see the glory itself," and after him Rabbi Simeon said much the same for all angels.

Of Jesus' belief in angels the Gospels leave us in no doubt. The Christian who cannot fit angels into his own notion of reality is left to explain it as an excusable error on the Saviour's part. Excusable or not, why must it have been an error? The assertion that there cannot be beings without material bodies is the most unprovable of dogmas—I had almost said the most improbable, but that would have been to intrude my own opinion.

To return to the world of men: Jesus makes one distinction between man and the material universe. "Heaven and earth will pass away, but my word will not" (Matthew 24.35). His word will not pass away not only because he who uttered it, but we for whom it was uttered, will not.

Before using the words I have quoted he had spoken of his own return in glory. Did he expect this to happen soon? On the idea that he did, quite a structure has been built. His followers, it is argued, expecting his immediate return—in a glory that they would share—settled down to wait in Jerusalem, with all the patience they could muster: owning all things in common (what did property matter with the curtain so soon to go up on a world made new?): making no effort to convert the Gentiles (for they would be but second-class citizens in the kingdom). But as time passed they had to re-think the situation. Christ kept on not coming, but the Gentiles came in increasing numbers. So the leaders put into Christ's mouth utterances like "Going teach all nations . . . and I am with you all days till the end of the world" (Matthew 28.20).

We have wondered what trust we could have in Gospels produced like that. This apart, did the first Christians expect the Parousia immediately? Most probably. Yet in the speeches of Peter after Pentecost, to the crowds and to the Sanhedrin, there is no hint of it. Did Jesus himself expect it? In the twenty-fourth chapter of Matthew we find him saying, "This generation shall not pass away till all these things take place," which suggests that it will be soon. What "this generation" was to see is not clear—the destruction of Jerusalem, perhaps, which was what the chapter is mainly about and which signified immeasurably more to him than it can to us. But of his own return in glory he says, "Of that day and hour no one knows, not even the angels of heaven, nor the Son, but the Father only."

This being the universe in which Jesus mentally, morally and emotionally lived, how does he see man's life? In his answer lies one of the greatest of all the differences he made, one of the greatest of his gifts to mankind. For he tells us what life is all about, and so makes it possible for us to handle ourselves and our world intelligently.

Left to ourselves, as we have noted, all we could actually know is that we are here, a little while ago we were not, a long time ago no one was, in a little while we shall not be. In other words, we could know that our life is a road, not a dwelling place. But why we are here—"why" meaning both *how* we get here and *for what purpose* if any—we have no means of knowing. Nor of ourselves have we any means of finding out why anything at all exists (why there isn't nothing), or where the road we are on leads, whether death is an end or a gateway, and if so to what.

Unless there is a Mind to account for the universe, there are of course no answers. The universe simply happened, and men are parts of the happening, as unmeant and unpurposed as it. But there is a Mind, and through Christ we can know what the Mind has in mind. We can know what life is about, we can try to live accordingly. It is a very great luxury.

To all this I have commonly met two reactions. The first is shrugged shoulders—what does it matter? My questioner can't imagine why I should see any great point in knowing what life is all about, his own ideas of luxury are of an earthier sort. Taking life as it comes, living towards nothing in particular, is OK with him. To me this seems sheerly retarded, sub-human. Cows give the same impression that they are concerned only with the patch of grass under their noses.

The other reaction is on a wholly different level. It

comes from men who do not question that such knowledge would be a great thing—they might even concede the word luxury—but cannot bring themselves to accept its possibility. They may face the impossibility of knowing with bleak pessimism, or they may find it no bar to their using life to the uttermost within the limits of their seeing.

Pessimism has no bleaker word than that life is "a tale told by an idiot, full of sound and fury, signifying nothing." I have heard this stated as Shakespeare's own answer to the riddle of life. But Shakespeare gave it as Macbeth's—it would be strange if he left his own profoundest comment on life to be uttered by a traitor and murderer, ghost-haunted and witch-haunted, in the moment of failure and death.

Those who are not thus reduced to a sense of futility choose goals for their actions based upon what they see as the good of humanity. But men equally dedicated see humanity's needs differently, and there is no way of deciding between them. I have used the phrase "community in fracture": this is the line of fracture. Only in agreement as to what man is and what life is about can it be healed.

The answer given by Christ is the only one on offer, it is a case of his answer or no answer. I am not saying that this is a reason for accepting his. But it is surely a reason for not rejecting it without the closest study of him and of it. God is at every point of Christ's answer. Genesis opens with "In the beginning God created the heavens and the earth." And Genesis tells us that God "created man in his own image, in the image of God he created him, male and female he created them . . . to have dominion over every living thing that moves upon the earth" (Genesis 1.27–28). God "formed man of the dust of the ground, and breathed into his nostrils the breath of life" (Genesis 2.7). And made man for friendship with Himself—the I-thou relationship was there from the beginning. So Genesis sees it. And Christ gives the chapter an authority the writer did not claim. Referring to the words of Genesis 2.24—"A man shall leave his father and mother and cleave to his wife, and two shall become one"—Christ says they are the words of God Himself—"who made them from the beginning and made them male and female" (Matthew 19.4–5).

God is at the beginning, willing men into existence, and by His will holding them in existence. And God is at the end; in fullness of union with Him men will reach the fullness of their own maturity and of union with their fellow men. If they choose.

2

Not to be aware of God, therefore, is not to be living in the real world. The old among my friends may remember a fable I once wrote about the man who regards the study of God as a harmless extra for those whose taste runs to religion but as not relevant to life's practicalities. In my fable you were riding in a car and warned the driver to swerve or he would hit a tree, and he answered, "It's no good talking to me about trees. I'm a motorist, not a botanist." You felt he was carrying respect for the rights of the specialist too far. A tree is not only a fact of botany, it is a fact. God is not only a fact of religion, He is a fact. It is not religious fanaticism but merely common sense to want to know what bearing a fact so vast has on us who depend for our very existence upon it.

But if the unspiritual man is surprised to hear us call God a fact, the hyper-spiritual man is pained. "Fact" comes from a Latin verb meaning to make, and God is not made. But etymology is an unsure guide to meaning: words can grow away from their roots (as plants cannot). For us the word "fact" means really existent, not an abstraction. But for the hyper-spiritual this explanation is not enough. Their Absolute is not exactly an abstraction but might as well be—its reality has nothing in common with any reality experienced by man. It is impenetrable by finite minds, inaccessible to our needs, touched by no care for our sufferings or sins. One wonders what grounds they have for seeing God so. Not in the Old Testament. Not in Christ.

Consider what he has to tell us about God in Himself. (In what follows there is an occasional sentence from my book *To Know Christ Jesus*.) He is the one only God, to be loved with all the power of mind and heart (Mark 12.44). He is good, He only is the Plenitude of goodness (Matthew 19.17). He is perfect—from that same Latin verb—(Matthew 5.48). All things are possible to him— even the salvation of the rich (Matthew 19.26). He is continuously in operation (John 5.44). He is the God of the living not the dead (Matthew 22.32). He is hidden, dwells in secret (Matthew 6.6). So far I have listed adjectives and verbs, he uses only one noun: "God is a spirit" (John 4.24), a phrase not to be found in the Old Testament.

And God is—one almost said naturally—concerned with, involved with, the universe He created. Jesus shows Him seeing, hearing, listening, answering, caring, loving, merciful, rewarding, punishing, forgiving (if men forgive), condemning their heartlessness, giving Himself, withdrawing Himself from those who refuse Him. He clothes the grasses of the field. No sparrow falls without God's knowledge.

Nor in all this is Jesus simply talking down to the inadequacy of men's minds. All that he says of God is clearly his own, so wholehearted is it, so spontaneous and matter-of-fact. He shows no trace of fretting at the limits of language, or even at the limits of human understanding. We observe that he makes all these same assumptions of God's concern for men when he speaks directly to God the Father. Take, for instance, his word from the Cross about his torturers—"Father, forgive them, for they know not what they do." This simply cannot be reconciled with divine inaccessibility or with the view that what a man does makes no difference. It means that God acts differently according to whether men do or do not realize the meaning of their own acts, and that His decisions can be affected by our asking Him.

The I-thou relation between God and men, which Genesis shows established at the very beginning of mankind's existence, reaches in Christ a depth of familiarity without parallel, and he wants a like familiarity to become habitual in us. His God and ours is not the impersonal God whose existence is at the end of a chain of argument, however flawless, or of an analysis of mystical experience, however overwhelming. He is not a problem to be solved, or a solution to be admired, but a reality to be known, loved, conversed with, contemplated, possessed, enjoyed. And in all these ways of contact there is no limit to the possibility of growth, as the Christian mystics have shown.

We do not find the actual phrase "God is love" on

Jesus' lips. It is in John's First Epistle. There is no question where John heard it. God loves men and wants to be loved by them. But what does it mean to love God? What *can* it mean?

The gulf between God our creator and ourselves, whom he created of nothing, is beyond measuring. But it does not doom us to ignorance of Him. Thomas Aquinas was paying tribute to the gulf by saying that we do not know what God is, only what He is not. But, as he knew, it was not what God is *not* who became man; and at the Last Supper Jesus did not answer Philip's request to be shown the Father by saying: "He that has seen me has seen what the Father is not."

The Fourth Council of the Lateran says more moderately that the unlikeness is greater than the likeness. This is indeed so: but it would also be true of you and your photograph—you being in three dimensions and it in two, you being flesh and blood and it light and shade on paper. Yet the photograph is recognizable. The likeness to Himself in which God made us *is* likeness. Christ has all sorts of ways of showing it, most notably I think by using the same words of God and man—spirit, life, knowledge, love, work—sometimes in the same sentence: "God is a *spirit* and they that worship him must worship him in *spirit* and in truth"; "No one *knows* the Father but the Son *and* him to whom the Son shall reveal him" (Luke 10.22); "If anyone *love* me, he will keep my word and the Father will *love* him." Our Lord could not have chosen a better way than this to show clearly that from our own knowledge of men we can proceed to a knowledge of God which is very far from negative.

The most surprising and therefore strongest word of

all for his purpose was "love." Left to himself no metaphysician would have thought of love as an attribute of God: if he had it would have been a very frigid love, with not much yearning in it. Paul tells us that Christ crucified was to the Greeks "foolishness" (1 Corinthians 1.23): about love of God they would have felt the same. Centuries earlier Aristotle had found a word more derisive still for what Christ was to give as the first of two key commandments: "It would be ridiculous," he said, "to talk of loving Zeus."

Once again we must be on our guard against fooling ourselves. We have heard the words "Love the Lord thy God" so often that we hardly hear the meaning any more. Do we in fact love God? What does "loving God" mean? None of the reactions we more or less automatically associate with love seem to apply to loving God— the desire for bodily contact, for instance, the stir within the emotions. We have noted that Christ does not define love but shows it in action. We show our love for people by what we do. At a point in time God showed His love for men by sending His Son—"He did not spare his own Son, but gave him up for us all." But from the beginning He had shown His love for men even more profoundly by wanting their love in return. Love is a reality deeper than the actions which flow from it. Love is in the will, willing the happiness of others, happy in their existence.

For love is cold if there is no emotional accompaniment at all. Analyzing this we shall agree, I think, that love involves a pleasure in the presence of the other, *a desire to be with*. Only once we hear Jesus speak of "loving" his Father (John 14.32). But without using the word love, he could say even more movingly: "I am not

alone, for my Father is with me." What of ourselves? We
have already questioned how much actual desire we
have to be with Christ Our Lord. Have we any desire at
all to be any closer to God than we are now? As a boy I
learnt a prayer, "Grant, O my God, that I may love and
enjoy You for ever in Heaven." I had been saying it for
years before I noticed the word "enjoy," and had to admit that I had never thought of God as enjoyable!

The minds of men have not often seen love as life's
meaning. Even those who are not led by the suffering in
it to rage against God, or deny Him altogether, do find
that it sets a question mark against His love—"Surely,"
they mumble to themselves, "He could do something
about it." They marvel at the assurance of St. John's
"God is love." He did not say it lightly. He had been in
Gethsemane when Christ begged his Father to remove
the chalice of suffering, and the suffering continued. He
was on Calvary when Christ cried out, "My God, my God,
why have you forsaken me?" But on Calvary also he had
heard Christ, dying, say, "Father, into your hands I commend my spirit." To know suffering unto desolation,
suffering unto death, yet not love God less, we must
somehow see the meaning of life as Christ saw it. And
that involves seeing God as Christ saw Him. How did he
see Him?

Chapter X

The God of Jesus

This book is about the difference Jesus makes. The greatest difference, the key to all the others as to his own view of reality, is in the God he unveils for us.

I

I have never met a man who started from total non-acceptance and arrived at the conviction that there is a God. Therefore I know nothing of the process by which such a man would arrive at the goal. Would he have travelled by any of St. Thomas's Five Ways, or by the ontological line of Anselm, Descartes, Leibnitz, or by the moral imperative of Kant? I have no means of knowing. But after all, we try to do this very thing ourselves —I mean that we try to prove God's existence by reason, with Faith excluded; and we offer the result to the unbeliever. In my experience he is not impressed by it.

But "prove," as the word is understood in English, is the wrong word. Arguments have value simply in clearing away obstacles that obscure vision. If they are successful, we find ourselves seeing the whole situation, *with the thing to be proved as an evident part of it.* There is something comparable in the drawings we occasionally see in children's magazines, drawings with a vast complication of lines, and the lines of a human face somewhere among them. Till you have discovered the face for yourself, you will be prepared to swear there isn't any face. But once you have seen it, then you can never again look at the picture without seeing it.

The line of thought which brought me to this kind of seeing of God begins with some truths so obvious that they seem hardly worth stating, so often stated that they no longer seem worth considering. People have heard them too often, and cannot believe that anything so familiar can possibly be light-bearing. But in a chaos, truisms come into their own; and our present religious condition *is* chaotic.

The first of our truisms is that if my parents had never met I should not have come into existence. When I think of all the myriad happenings from the beginning of the world which might have prevented them from existing, to say nothing of meeting, I realize how chancy my own arrival on this earth was. And this chanciness —philosophers call it contingency—is not peculiar to me. It is hard to think of anything now existing that might not just as easily have not existed, if things earlier had fallen out differently.

The second of these obvious truths is that contingency will not account for everything. If there is nothing at all that could exist unless some other thing had been as it was, or happened as it did, then the process would never have got started, so to speak. If everything whatsoever had to owe its existence to something else's having been or happened, what something *is* there outside everything whatsoever? To me it seems that there has to be something which simply exists, exists in its own right, independently of what any other thing does

—something self-existent, in fact. It must be a rich full-ness of existence, for there can be nothing in the uni-verse—life, power, knowledge, will—that does not in some way derive from it.

I offer all this not as a "proof," but as the way I came to see the face of Self-Existence. I marvelled that there were those whom I could not bring to see it. But then, of course, I had already accepted it. Before embarking on the effort to establish God's existence by reason with no aid from faith, I had had twenty years of Catholic life. I saw God as Christ had shown Him to me; I had been trying to do His will; I had been reacting to Him—very varied reactions, with not much reason for pride in any of them, reason for shame in some of them; I had an awareness of His majesty, an awareness of my own meagreness; my certainty of Him had grown to include certainty of His certainties. All these things I had, in a cloudy mixture perhaps; but they added up to a life I had been living and found real, a life with its own vital laws—laws which brought the conviction of their valid-ity when I obeyed them, and a new and more intense conviction when I disobeyed.

When for the first time I met the idea that if anything at all exists there must be a Self-Existent being, I re-joiced in it; but it did not make me any surer of God's existence than I already was. If at some future time I should come to question its validity, my acceptance of God would not be weakened: for that is based upon two facts which lie outside the argument, namely, the cer-tainty that Christ lived by it, and my own experience of living by it. The argument simply cannot have the same effect upon one who must consider it without the sup-port of two facts so compelling.

All the same the purely intellectual way seems to me sound and true. For one who already believes, it sheds new light upon God Himself and upon our relation to Him. For one who does not believe, it is a useful massaging of the intellect—raising questions, opening vistas—so that he is better equipped for the contact with God and His Christ which alone can be decisive.

For the Western world today the problem is whether God exists. That was not the question asked by the world into which Christ came. Divinity was universally accepted there, the writers of neither Testament show any sign of having ever met a serious atheist. The "fool" who "said in his heart there is no God" was no philosopher denying God's existence but a corrupt man counting on not being punished by God. And "fool" was all the answer the Psalmist found it necessary to give. He did not try to provide an argument which had only to be stated to put God's existence beyond question. Nor did Jesus.

It is worth our while to glance back at our distant ancestors and their religion. We have a way of speaking as if they invented gods to account for whatever in nature they found inexplicable: but little by little the area of the unexplained has shrunk before the discoveries of science. We now know that thunder is not a tyrant god roaring his rage, rain is not a fertility god pouring down semen. And it was in the area of the unexplained, we tell ourselves, that the need for God was felt: it was His country, so to speak: and now where is it? And where is He?

Basic to the myths was the certainty that the seen, heard, felt, smelt world was not all there is. Behind it, or beyond it, or interpenetrating it, was another reality, unseen, unheard, unfelt, unsmelt. There was no question of proving it, it was simply there, as much as the world of sense. What the primitive made of the relation between the seen and the unseen we can only guess. But for those who believe in the unseen, the certainty that there *is* a relation does not depend upon ignorance of science. A hundred years after Newton, Wordsworth could write of

> . . . something far more deeply interfused,
> Whose dwelling is the light of setting suns. . . .

It did not occur to the far from primitive Egyptians or Sumerians or Babylonians or Canaanites to apply to a myth the tests that belong to the sense-world. It was sufficient for them that they felt their life richer because of it. For the answers science has found are not to the questions which caused men to turn to God or the gods: nor do they touch the needs which, in varying measures, men found met by religion. If we consider the contacts with God men sought and found in the Old Testament—its first books written three thousand years ago—it is clear that the discoveries of science have no bearing on them at all.

There is the loneliness and lostness of the creature in the vastness of the universe, panic in the heart at the evil all about us, sickness in the heart at the evil in oneself. It would never occur to a reader of the Old Testament that Adam's problem, or Cain's, or Jacob's, or David's, Jeremiah's or Hosea's would have been met if only they could have had our knowledge of astronomy and biology and psychology. For with all that we know, we find their difficulties are still ours. On every page of the Old Testament we meet ourselves, our astronomically, biologically, psychologically erudite selves—but with nothing like our suicide rate. Resisting the temptation to speculate on the curious fact that the most scientific age the world has known is so very suicidal, we may at least remind ourselves once more of two questions science cannot answer.

The first—why anything at all exists, Why isn't there nothing?—cannot be answered by scientific investigation of what happens to the universe once it exists. With this unanswered, the claim to have reduced the area of the unexplained is less impressive. This first question of course concerns only the man of intellectual appetite, the easily satisfied can decide not to ask it. But the second is of the most intense practicality for everyone. Neither science nor philosophy can tell man what life is all about—why he is here, what value he has, whether death is the end, what, if anything, comes next for the individual or the race. With these questions left hanging, it is mockery to talk of a world already made explicable by science, or on the way to being made so.

We can know the answers to either of our questions only if there is a God *and He communicates with us.* Without such a communication, the most gifted scientist or philosopher is no nearer knowing them than the least gifted cave man who ever clubbed the wrong woman. God *has* communicated in many ways, especially through the prophets, most richly in Christ.

2

Jesus was born in, and born of, the Middle East. Before him stretched a long religious history, forty centuries of it, from the Sumerians with their high god

Enki and the Babylonians with Marduk, whom his ancestors had worshipped (Joshua 24.2). Into that history, twelve hundred years before Jesus, had thrust the new religious fact of Israel, made into a people by Moses, established in Canaan by Joshua.

I call it new, and by the time it had shaken free of certain ancestral habits and settled down as itself, it was almost totally so. There is nothing to compare with it among the religions of mankind. In two matters especially it is unique. Its history is written, as no other nation's history has been, entirely as the story of its relation with God. And this God, Yahweh, was One—Babylon counted its gods in their thousands. Reading the opening chapters of Genesis is like waking from a nightmare into daylight.

The deepest reason for the difference between Israel and the great paganisms is that these formed their religion, gods and all, out of their experience of the natural universe, the Jews got theirs from their experience of God in the Desert. Scholars may question details of the Desert Experience, but certainly something happened there three thousand years ago whose influence has lived on, through Jews and Christians and Mohammedans, till now. It shows no signs of dying. In some way God spoke to them, the communication was statable and preservable in words. And the words made the difference.

In our own day verbal revelation is flipped aside as "statement," "proposition," and God is held to reveal Himself only in the natural universe and the history of man. But this is back to Babylon. All psychology, we say, is projection—in every human situation we read ourselves and our reactions and judge accordingly. All theology is projection too, unless God has spoken. If men can know God only as revealed in nature and man, then either they will not recognize Him at all: or they will see God simply as man writ large, man writ immense—in fact themselves rewritten as God.

So with the Babylonians. Like us, they valued power and sex: so their gods were monsters of cruelty (the goddesses especially) and madly oversexed. The god our age finds for itself will not be a monster of cruelty—we have the long Judaeo-Christian education to make that improbable. Will he be obsessed with sex? Probably. If there is a new religion it will honor its god's sexuality with sex rituals. But the God of the Old Testament differed from the gods of paganism by having no consort! Genesis places sex firmly where it belongs, not in God but in human life. Even the truth that God had a Son of His own could not safely be revealed to a world in which the Greek god Uranus was castrated by his son Zeus, the Canaanite god El by his son Baal.

Such crudities our age will avoid: if men invent a god he will express themselves at their best. But he will not be the God of Jesus Christ. For between God as He is and any god men may make in their own image God has placed words. After all man is a word-making, word-using animal: his mastery of the universe would be impossible without words. It would be strange if God, communicating with men, should ignore the most specifically human element in them. It is true, of course, that words cannot be adequate to express infinite reality: they must always be shallower than God, but they are not shallower than we and they can take us out of our shallows.

The word of God, the speech of God, is all over the

Old Testament. Whether God had "said" those individual words to the prophets and the others, or had simply given them the light and strength to see the divine reality so and utter it so, He wanted us to have the words. Indeed we have seen that one great phrase of Genesis—"man and wife become one flesh"—which we might have read either as Adam's welcome to Eve or as the writer's comment on marriage, is quoted by Jesus as God's (Matthew 19.5).

The words of revelation are essential. In their light we see with new richness the God revealed in His creation: and they are a check on our tendency to re-make Him in our own image, as the Babylonians made him in theirs. So it seems to me. So it seemed to Jesus. He quoted the words of Deuteronomy, "Man does not live by bread alone but by every word that proceeds from the mouth of God." And he emphasizes the importance of his own words—"The words I have spoken to you are spirit and life" (John 6.63)—and their permanence—"Heaven and earth will pass away, but my words will not pass away" (Luke 21.33). You can, if you will, ignore "statement" and "proposition"; but Scripture does not, Christ did not.

The God of Jesus Christ is a loving father, but for neither the love nor the fatherhood did men have to wait for Christ's revelation. The Old Testament has both in rich measure. It has fatherhood, of course—"Like as a father pities his children, so the Lord has compassion on those who fear him" (Psalm 102.15). It has motherhood too—God will no more forget Israel than "a mother can forget her infant, the son of her womb" (Isaiah 49.15)—you will not easily surpass that in the New Testament. What could Christ add to a God whose love is already expressed so movingly?

That he does add something the Christian feels overwhelmingly. Most of us have had the same experience in our reading of the Old Testament—there are times when we feel Our Lord's presence, times when we feel his absence almost physically. The truth is that in their intimacy with God the Jews were growing, growing towards a fullness they could not yet know or even conceive. In this as in so much else the Old Testament is foreshadowing, reaching out for, someone to come, with no notion of the greater uses to which its own great words would one day be put.

The growing was at incredible speed. It was out of centuries of slavery in Egypt that Moses brought his people, and slavery is not educational, mentally or religiously. In a couple of centuries after their settling down in Canaan they had reached the level of Samuel and David and Solomon. Four or five hundred years before the Incarnation the Psalm of Creation in Genesis I, written it would seem as a Preface to the Pentateuch, formulated and uttered a theological statement profounder than men had ever known. The next paragraph is from the summary I made of it in *Genesis Regained:*

"God was Someone, not just a force; He was distinct from the universe, as against Pantheism; the powers of nature, all living things, were His creatures (it is hard for us to imagine how shocked millions must have been to find the sun, their supreme god, casually brought into the picture half way through the week as a convenience thought up for man by Israel's God). He was one, as against the myriad polytheisms; evil was not a separate creative principle, as dualism held, it was not given a place in the universe as God produced it; the universe as it came from God was 'very good'—this against the vast Eastern tendency to regard matter either as evil or as illusion. And man was to be earth's Lord—no myth had ever approached that."

I talked in an earlier chapter of ancestral elements Israel needed to shed. There was cruelty, for instance: it was long before they ceased to assume in Yahweh the habit of slaughter common in all their world. I cannot remember that Jesus ever quotes any Old Testament text that shows God demanding bloodshed. And there was the nature of God's relation to themselves: every people had its own special god, Israel's was Yahweh. Only slowly the realization came that He alone was God, the rest no more than men's imaginings. Even more lingeringly died the conviction that He was their property, so to speak—they of course must not go whoring after other gods, but for Him to love other peoples as He loved them would have been a kind of adultery.

God's desire for men's love is the specifying element of the Old Testament. Like the gods of the pagans Yahweh demanded obedience, but none of the paganisms show their gods commanding love, almost begging for it, as He does. Love was the one gift the Infinite wanted of men, the one gift the weakest could refuse the omnipotent.

The impersonal Absolute, which the Greeks were to get from India, which has fascinated Christian thinkers throughout the centuries and has taken hold of so many of our own today, is not in the Old Testament or in the New. Throughout both, God knows, loves, intervenes, God wants to be known, to be loved, to be prayed to intervene! "Your father who knows in secret will reward you in secret"—that is Jesus talking, but his listeners would hardly have found it novel.

Reading the Old Testament, we cannot escape God's fatherhood. His care for His people is continually compared with a father's, and we are not meeting only a figure of speech. Yet we sometimes wonder if the ancient Jewish father-image was quite ours, or Christ's: we remember "He who spares the rod hates his son." Between the two Testaments anyhow, there is a certain difference of "feel," and I think it is to be found precisely in the matter of God's fatherhood. When Our Lord tells the disciples "Many prophets and kings have desired to see what you have seen and have not seen it," he has just talked of the Father. And the new truth he revealed was very novel indeed. So read Luke 10.17–23.

3

The God, then, whom Jesus found in the religion into which he was born was a loving Father. At school he was taught the Song of Moses—"Is not he your father who created you?" (Deuteronomy 32.6)—and he found the same idea in Malachi, the latest of the prophets: "Have we not all one father, has not God created us?" (2.10). In Psalm 44 he would have met "As the stag pants for the fountain of waters, my soul pants for thee, O God. My soul has thirsted for the strong, living God"—such an anguished cry of longing for God is not to be matched in the New Testament, yet to both Fatherhood and Love Jesus was to give not only new light and depth but a reality not dreamed of.

In the New Testament there is a multitudinousness in the utterance of the fatherhood. Between the Fourth Gospel and his three Epistles John has "Father" close on ninety times. Before him (a whole generation before, perhaps) come Matthew, Mark and Luke—they use the word not with the same frequency, but it is they who give us some of those uses which have most pierced men's souls. Mark has "Abba, Father, remove this cup from me, yet not what I will but what you will" (14.36). Luke has "Father, forgive them, for they know not what they do" (23.44), and "Father, into your hands I commend my spirit" (23.46). Matthew has "Baptizing them in the name of the Father and of the Son and of the Holy Spirit" (28.19). Matthew and Luke both give us the Lord's prayer, the Our Father. Before the Gospels most of the Epistles came, with the word Father in a profusion approaching John's. Those first Christians could hardly think of God without remembering that He was their Father, and they revelled in uttering the word. How strong is that excitement in us?

It was not a matter of frequency only, though the frequency is significant: there is what the word Father was now saying. Jesus not only speaks *of* God and *to* God as Father, which we hear no prophet or Psalmist of old doing, but he urges us to do so too. He has gone beyond Moses' and Malachi's seeing of God as father because as creator He is the source of life (which is paternity's essence, of course); he has gone beyond God's having created man in His own image and likeness (which is close to paternity's definition). He who made all things new did not exclude our sonship of God. In revealing his own eternal sonship he created a new sonship for men.

We have already looked at the account Luke gives (10.17) of the welcome Christ gave the seventy-two disciples on their return from their mission to the cities of Israel. It is the solitary occasion on which we are told that Jesus was joyful: "He rejoiced in the Holy Spirit and said, 'I thank you, Father, Lord of heaven and earth, because you have hidden these things from the wise and prudent and revealed them to little ones.' " Then comes, "All things have been delivered to me by my Father," followed by the supreme statement he was to make about the relation of Father and Son within the Godhead: *"No one knows* the Son but the Father, and no one knows the Father but the Son and him to whom the Son shall reveal him." John's Gospel could shed light upon this but could not add to it.

It was no mere rhetorical exaggeration that something unknown to the "wise and prudent" of Israel was being revealed to these nobodies. Jesus repeats it: "Many prophets and kings desired to see and hear what you see and hear and did not see it, did not hear it." God is not only Father of men: there was fatherhood and sonship within God Himself. There is a unique balance of being between Father and Son, expressed in a unique balance of inter-knowledge.

With all the splendor surrounding it, the utterance itself has a simple matter-of-factness, not as of one saying something which (as Newman said of pious exaggerations about Our Lady) can be explained only by being explained away. The Son knows the Father as the Father knows him. But he is not hugging the knowledge jealously to himself: he has come to enrich our knowledge with his. Not only that: he has come as our brother to enrich our sonship with his. When the new Christians addressed God as Father it was in the knowledge that God was a Father with a Son of His own, and that by that Son their own sonship had been lifted to a new level.

We have come back more than once to Jesus' first revelation that within the very being of God there were two selves, each knowing himself as himself, each knowing the Other as Other: that the second of these selves, God's Son, now moved among men as Man. They had called him the Son of God, now he revealed to them that this was no mere title of glory which might have made him unique among men, but no more than man. It is quite literally a first unveiling of the innermost life of God. In the later books of the Old Testament, written in Greek by Jews formed on Greek philosophy, there was a feeling towards it, but that is all.

Those spiritual ancestors of ours made no enquiry into what God's own life might be—what He was doing, say, when He wasn't intervening in the affairs of the Jews. Indeed we can hardly blame them if they felt that keeping the Israelites on the straight path and bringing them back from their endless wanderings was quite enough occupation even for an omnipotent God. Whatever the reason, they did not use their minds upon Him *as Himself.* What Paul says (1 Corinthians 2.10) of "the depths of God which the Spirit searches" would not have meant much to them before this utterance of Christ's.

They would have known it as blasphemy to deny that He was all-powerful, all-knowing, eternal—but they had not pierced into these words: they could not, having given no full thought to the notion of spirit. When we hear Christ say to the Samaritan woman at the well, "God is a Spirit," we glide over it as a cliché. In fact the phrase is not in the Old Testament. That God's Son should want to reveal to us the inner life of God is a more certain proof of love even than his dying for us. One may sacrifice all one has for others, even life itself, out of mercy or compassion or even a sense of duty. But only love wants to know and be known.

Readers may feel that I am wasting too much time on Christ's unveiling of God. I can almost hear the word relevance being whispered by even the friendliest. The living of our lives here on earth is what matters to us, why don't I concentrate on what difference Jesus of Nazareth makes to that, instead of keeping readers drifting in the desert of abstract theology? But if one believes in God at all—if only as the reason why anything, including ourselves, exists—it would be odd not to want to know everything available about Him. Nothing could be less abstract than the reason for everything, nothing more relevant.

Whether or not we see it so, Jesus saw it so. He knew himself as coming from the Father to bring us to the Father. If we want to find out what he has for us, we must look long and closely at what matters to him. If what matters to him does not matter to us, why bother about him at all? It may be regrettable that he attaches so much importance to God, when we want to hear about ourselves. Be patient. We'll get to "relevance" soon enough—i.e., our living of our own lives! Meanwhile we must occupy ourselves a little longer with his living of his.

I spoke in the last chapter of the mind we bring to the reading of the Gospels. In what follows, concerning Trinity and Incarnation, my own mind has been nourished by a particular theological teaching. I shall do my best to draw no meaning from the texts that is not there. I hope, with all diffidence, that even those whose interpretation of any text differs, will see how I have arrived at mine.

For this first unveiling is a milestone in his own life. None of the prophets of Israel had ever claimed to know God. What must it have meant to a carpenter from Galilee to make such a claim, and not only about God but about himself in relation to God? More profoundly, what must it have meant to him that it was true?

Even of those who do not accept the doctrines of Trinity and Incarnation the vast majority feel that Jesus is unique, not as other men, in some way Man Plus. They, and we who believe, try to analyze the Plus, to cope mentally with it! But what must it have meant to him to have to *be* it, to cope with it in daily living? What must it have meant to have to utter it—knowing that, to begin with, his followers would not make head or tail of it?

What it did mean to him we cannot actually know, since he does not tell us. But in Matthew's account of the same revelation (II.25–30), we learn that after it Jesus, in the clearest utterance he has left us of his love, told what it would mean to men: "Come to me all who labor and are heavy burdened, and I will give you rest. Take my yoke upon you and learn from me, for I am gentle and lowly in heart, and you shall find rest for your souls."

4

Jesus told of a Father and Son within the Godhead, two selves linked in a mutual knowledge shared by none other, and himself that Son. What it meant to him to utter it we are not told. What it meant to the disciples we are not told either—no very full comprehension, probably. We do know that when he made the eating of his flesh and drinking of his blood a condition of eternal life (John 6) they were as shocked as the rest. That time Peter spoke for them all—save one perhaps. In answer to Christ's sad question, "Will you leave me too?" he said, "To whom else shall we go? You have the words of eternal life."

But this assertion of two selves within God must have sounded more instantly shocking, as blasphemy is more shocking than mystery. At least since the return from captivity in Babylon, the Jews were monotheists to the marrow of their bones. We know from John (8.59 and 10.31) that on two occasions when the Jews suspected Jesus of teaching a duality of gods, they took up stones to slay him.

Short of that, what could the disciples have thought he was saying? The pagan gods were forever fathering offspring, but then they were carnality itself: there was no carnality in Israel's God. What could it mean that God, a spirit, should have a son?

One of the Twelve who heard Jesus utter the words was to open up a way into that particular mystery. John begins his Gospel with "In the beginning was the Word, and the Word was with God, and the Word was God." Writing in Greek, he used "Logos" for Word. His older contemporary, the Alexandrian Jew Philo, had used "logos" in a different sense. He would have found meaningless and indeed revolting John's statement a few verses further on that "the Word was made flesh"—revolting because flesh was a degradation for spirit, meaningless because his own "logos" was not Someone, but only something.

Such a vast amount has been written about "the Johannine Logos," that one would hardly realize that John barely mentions it. As I wrote in *God and the Human Mind,* "We might get the impression that John was wholly logos-minded, logos-soaked, perhaps converted to the logos in some Patmos vision, as possessed by it as Paul by his experience on the Damascus road. In fact, John mentions it only twice, here and in his First Epistle; and he gives no indication of why he uses it at all. He never discusses the concept or draws anything from it. From Word he passes within a few verses to Son, and Son it remains for the rest of the Gospel. One wonders if he might not just as well have said, 'In the beginning was the Son, and the Son was with God, and the Son was God.' "

Why did John use Word if he was going to make no use of it? I cannot pretend to read his mind, but at least we can see what light it shed upon how God, a spirit, could have a Son.

To quote *God and the Human Mind* again, "God utters a Word, a mental Word evidently, not framed by the mouth, more akin to an Idea. And this Word is God. Of what could God conceive an Idea which would *be* God? Not of any created thing certainly, not of all creation in its totality, only of Himself." The Idea is wholly adequate. It not only represents the original as spirit, infinite, eternal, divine, as all-knowing, all-loving, all-powerful. The Idea *is* all these things, for the Idea is God.

What God is telling us is that within the One God there are two Persons, two selves, each knowing Himself for Himself: One giving totally, the Other receiving totally: each God, One by origin, the Other by gift. "One who has brought his mind to bear upon the Thinker conceiving an Idea of Himself will find less difficulty in applying to God the process of a father begetting a son. In our own human experience both processes, thinking and begetting, are ways of producing likeness. The First Person begets a son by His generative power as a father begets, conceives a son within his own being as a mother conceives. All parenthood is in the birth of this first son, generation and conception in one single, eternal act."

How much of this was in the mind of John or Paul or any of them we do not know. In the Epistles, Jesus is the Son, Jesus is Kyrios—the Greek word with which the Septuagint translates Yahweh.

With this second Self we get the beginning of the answer to a problem which has always nagged at men even though they might not have been able to put it into words. They have always shrunk away from the Solitary God, companionless in eternity. Polytheism was one way of escape, the Impersonal Absolute was another. We now have Companionship within the Deity, two who could love and be loved infinitely.

5

With two Selves within the One God, as we have noted, Jesus was trying the Twelve high. And two was not the end of it. They were to hear of a Third, called Pneuma—the Breath—which we have come to translate as Spirit. In the breathing forth of the love of Father and Son, Christian theology since Augustine has seen the origin of that Third. Infinite knowledge had produced an Idea that was Someone, infinite love was no less productive.

Karl Rahner counts forty-four occasions in the New

Testament where the one God is spoken of in Three terms. Forty years before John wrote his Gospel, Paul uses this triplicity again and again. The formula we know best, "Father, Son and Holy Spirit," occurs only once, and in Matthew, not in John. Near the end of his time on earth Jesus tells his apostles to baptize "into the name of the Father, and of the Son, and of the Holy Spirit" (28.19–20). Otherwise the terms vary—the First of the Three is Father, or simply God; the Second is Son or Lord; but the Third is, always and only, Spirit.

After nineteen hundred years of it, Catholics are so accustomed to the Trinity, three Persons in One God, that when they meet the Holy Spirit in Matthew, Mark and Luke it may not occur to them that if we had only these three Gospels it would not be easy to show the Spirit as a distinct Person. In John's Gospel we find the Spirit called "He"—which is strange enough, since the Greek word *pneuma* is neuter. But the chances are it does not strike us that this is something we had not heard from the other three Evangelists.

In the Old Testament the Spirit of God was simply God in his actions upon men. In the Synoptic Gospels too the Spirit is always in action, always doing something —at the very origin of Christ, for instance, it is by the Spirit's power that the Virgin conceives (Luke 1.35); and at the origin of the Church, the Spirit comes upon the Apostles as Christ had promised (Acts 1). After the Baptism in Jordan, the Spirit "drove Jesus out into the wilderness." The Temptations over, "Jesus returned in the power of the Spirit into Galilee." By the Spirit, Jesus says he casts out demons (Matthew 12.28). When the disciples returned he "rejoiced in the Holy Spirit." Always the dynamism of the Spirit is in him and with him.

The same linking of the Holy Spirit with power, action, we find again and again in the Acts and the Epistles. At Pentecost the Spirit gave the Apostles utterance, gave it likewise to the first martyr, Stephen. The Spirit said, "Separate me Saul and Barnabas for the work to which I have called them," told Philip to approach the eunuch whom in due course he baptized, directed Peter to the reception of the Gentile Cornelius. And so on. The Acts are the Gospel of the Holy Spirit as the Four Gospels are Christ's.

That this Third One is shown us as divine is beyond question. Is he a distinct person? Outside John it would be hard to find a single Gospel text which could mean only that. But Paul gives us the mysterious assurance "The Spirit himself intercedes for us with sighs too deep for words." The Church in fact has always seen him as a Third Person. If the first Christians did not see him so, then the forty-four occurrences of the three terms, all a generation or more before John wrote, are hard to explain. Clearly they knew that the Unity needs to be expressed as in some way Three. The Spirit is always there and, to quote myself, "if he is not divine as Father and Son are, his invariable presence is meaningless, almost embarrassingly, as of one who does not belong but cannot be left out!"

One puzzling thing Jesus says, all the more puzzling because we find it in Matthew (12.31), not John: "Every sin and blasphemy will be forgiven men, but the blasphemy against the Holy Spirit will not be forgiven. Whoever says a word against the Son of Man will be forgiven, but whoever speaks against the Holy Spirit will not be forgiven either in this age or the age to come." The notion of an unforgivable sin seems to contradict Jesus' own words, "He who comes to me I will not turn away." Whatever the sin is, its unforgivableness must arise from something in its own nature. Perhaps, given that the Holy Spirit subsists by the way of love, the sin against Him is the refusal of love: and this, unrepented, makes union with God impossible.

Chapter XI

The Identity of Jesus

There is no way of making sense of man's earthly life as a short story complete in one instalment. This had already been shown in Ecclesiastes better than I could show it, in Job better than anyone has ever shown it. My advantage over both is that they had no real notion of what other instalment there might be. They could only cling to the certainty that God is over all. Whatever the sufferings of life, God must—blindly, often enough—be trusted, God must be obeyed.

It was for Christ to bring light to the blindness, or rather full light to the half-light, in which all the Old Testament is wrapped. Once he had unveiled God's own personal life, the supreme phrase "God is love" could at last be uttered: with that God, Christ shows that we can have union here on earth to the limit of our willingness —any refusal is ours, there is no refusal in God: and he shows what the next instalment of our life can be in union with God and so with all men who have not refused him. For refusal remains to every man a possibility. Salvation is no automatic machinery

> To pack and label men for God,
> And save them by the barrel-load.

145

Acceptance or refusal is for each of us.

Ecclesiastes accepts, Job accepts, obedience as the sole rule of life in a suffering world. There is fascination for us in the mysterious statement of Hebrews (5.8) that Jesus too, Son as he was, learnt obedience from the things he suffered. However it may have been for him, obedience is the last thing most of us learn. With all that we know and Job did not, it still calls for a vast effort on God's part and a vast response on ours, to bring us to the instinctive awareness that the powers of this world will be hostile, the promises of this world futile—that, as Chesterton saw,

> The Devil is a gentleman
> And never keeps his word.

You may be surprised that I should thus suddenly drag in the Devil. My immediate excuse is that I enjoy that particular quotation. But my deepest reason is that Satan is a convenient instance of a modern attitude to Christ as revealer, which puts a vast question mark over all I have so far written in this chapter—and indeed over all that Christ said and did.

What I have in mind is the tendency to choose in the Gospels whatever one happens to agree with, and either explain away the rest or placidly ignore it, as though it were politer to Christ to act as if he hadn't said or done it. . . . I have just finished reading an article on Satan, written by a Catholic. The writer does not believe that there is any such person. But he admits that Jesus did. Now it might seem that if a Christian decides to differ from Christ, some explanation is called for: he can hardly, one would think, say Christ believed in Satan but I don't, and leave it at that. Yet that in effect is what our writer does.

In a long article, the fact that to Jesus, Satan was a real person gets exactly four sentences. Two of these concede the fact, a third remarks that readers of simple faith may believe it, the fourth that Scripture scholars are not clear as to what Satan means but can in fact account satisfactorily for evil without him. Christ's belief thus by-passed, the writer can spread himself happily on his own disbelief—but with not a word to show why a personal spirit of evil could not exist. The whole article was as cool an example as I have seen of what I have called a placid ignoring of Jesus by a Christian—most make some effort to find a new interpretation of his words which will save his credibility!

I have dwelt on this particular matter at length not because it is about Satan but because it illustrates in reverse the principle on which this book is written—namely that we must grow in knowledge of the Jesus *of the Gospels.* First find out what the Evangelists record him as saying or doing. If you feel you must reinterpret, at least know what the original is in which you are finding a new meaning. If you feel you cannot accept it at all, at least know what you are denying. But in that event think out what your own relation is to Jesus as Revealer, to Jesus as Redeemer. On what he means to us, we dare not fool ourselves. We have no choice but to try to find out who and what Jesus thought he was, his identity in fact.

I

"Contemporary man cannot accept"—that phrase has a finality about it never known before, especially as a factor in Gospel study. Who is contemporary man whose ability to accept is so decisive? Not you, I imagine, not I certainly: probably he is the writer himself, feeling it politer to say "contemporary man" instead of "I and people of my sort." Whoever he is, it is agreed by those who have invented him, that he "cannot accept a transcendent God whom he has never experienced." So the God that Jesus did appear to accept must be explained away—as a Jewish tradition perhaps, which the Galilean Carpenter either found it convenient to use, or had himself not outgrown.

We believe—"contemporary man cannot"—that the original being exists because what it is demands existence, it exists therefore in its own right, it cannot nonexist, it is wholly independent, not needing anything else to be or happen in order to make it be. Let us admit that such a being is hard to conceive: but it is not more so than a universe which simply happened to be there for no reason at all, external to itself or internal. *Either way something beyond our understanding is at the origin of things.*

We believe, and contemporary man apparently cannot, that intelligence and will were at the origin of the universe. As intelligence and will are in the universe now, there is nothing especially progressive about denying their presence at its source: it would seem at least more probable than that they emerged as the result of mindless atoms bashing about through billions of years: more probable than that the immeasurably complex inter-relatedness of our universe (which all have experienced) should merely have happened, unmeant, unwilled, by chance, in the course of the same blind bashing of atoms.

It is also agreed that contemporary man is in search of his identity, who he is, what he is, why he matters. If there is no intelligent being at the origin of the universe, then mankind emerged unpurposed, unmeant. Each individual remains above the surface of matter for a while, then is once more re-merged in it. Mindlessness has the last word over every one of us. What can "identity" mean for such a being, with no past, no future, so precarious a present? The only ones who could have "purposed" him are his parents, and no contemporary man would dream of finding out what *their* purpose was, and living by that! In any event each individual has to face the question whether, with a population growing beyond the earth's power to feed it, he ought to exist at all: was it not wrong of his parents to have him? He may well be tempted, like Job, to curse the day he was born, or as Chesterton put it

> To curse the day whereon his body and soul
> Escaped the vigilance of birth control

The embarrassing possibility that he may indeed have arrived as an unwelcome side-effect of the pill, or as the result of a test-tube mating of which his parents knew nothing, must affect the meaning and the value of the identity he is searching for. But wrapping it all is the mindless, meaningless, purposeless universe in which he exists so transiently.

If contemporary man will not accept the transcendent God without whom the universe has no meaning, then it is he who must explain himself, not Jesus. He has turned out the light and must pursue his search for his identity in the dark, until the dark swallows him as it has swallowed the myriads of men before him.

Jesus accepted the God of Israel, whose intelligence and will had brought the universe into being, in whose image and likeness men are made. That God he unveiled for us, showing that within the oneness of limit-less Existence there was a personal life of limitless knowledge and limitless love—the knowledge and the love, like the existence, were each not only something, as they are in men, but Someone.

Men were not left with the mixed swarm of gods that the pagans had, or the impersonal god of the philosophers, or even with Israel's majestic hidden God, whose inner life was sealed to them. And Jesus showed God as not only the source of man's existence but the goal—men were to grow to their individual completeness, mankind to its perfection as community, in a fullness of union with Him that would never cease.

In the context of reality as Jesus revealed it, identity has meaning—for us, and for him. The discovery of our own identity is enriched in the discovery of his. We must search for his.

The search for the identity of Jesus goes on and on. At a turning point in his mission he asked the Apostles "Who do you say I am?" (Matthew 16.19). With that question he still challenges men. Even those who wholly reject him cannot leave him and his identity alone.

But in all this seething of intellectual energy, what Jesus himself gave as the first rule for the enquiry—the doing of God's will—is not much in evidence. Is his teaching from God, or is he simply delivering a message of his own? "A man will know," he says, "provided his will is to do God's will" (John 7.17). But today a man may believe that God's will cannot be known, or that God has no will, or that there is no God, without any diminution of his influence as a Scripture scholar.

The one essential is that he must know the documents. There is an astonishing importance attached to their writtenness! It might be assumed, for instance, that when John, in obedience to Christ's words from the cross, "took Mary to his own home," their daily conversation was not only about the people next door. They must have discussed Jesus, whom they knew as no other two knew him. Particularly they must have talked of Sonship, which had such a unique meaning for each of them. But in discussing John's Gospel this is never mentioned because there is no documentary evidence. The influence on John of Philo is discussed lengthily but not the influence of Mary—all because John uses one word "logos" which is also used by Philo (in a different sense). Along with this excessive respect for the written word goes what looks like its exact opposite—what *is* written must submit to each scholar's judgment of what is historically, exegetically, psychologically possible: and whatever survives judgment so rigorous must be further tested as to its spiritual relevance to the needs of today.

At least, you say, the documents are read. They are indeed, but all the same we are sometimes startled at what the scholars think they find in them. All four Gospels begin their account of Jesus' public life with John the Baptist, Jesus' baptism by him, and the descent of the Holy Spirit in the form of a dove; and all but John give the voice from heaven greeting Jesus as Son. Here are three comments I have read: "Only after the Baptism did he begin to be afraid as he saw the opposition growing." "Only after the Baptism did he know he was doomed." "Baptism seems to have marked a turning point in Jesus' awareness of his relation to his Father." Note the words, "Only after the Baptism" and "turning point." You would never guess that the Baptism is quite literally the first appearance on the stage of the adult Jesus. Before it we know nothing whatever of what he thought, felt, was aware of, knew or feared. All we have is the answer of the twelve-year-old to his mother in the Temple—"Didn't you know that I must be about my Father's business?" This suggests a pretty formed "awareness of his relation to his Father." The men I have quoted did not believe that particular incident happened, of course; but then they do not believe in the voice from heaven either, for all that they make it a turning point. Take out the voice and the dove and not much is left of Epiphany.

The writers in fact bring their own image of Jesus to the Gospels and find it in them. I dwell on this, as on earlier obliquities, as a warning to ourselves. We are all in the same danger of reading into the Gospels what fits our ideas, and reading out of them what doesn't.

Before their account of John the Baptist, two of the Gospels have a kind of Prologue, mainly concerned with the virginal conception of Jesus, Matthew telling of how this was made known by an angel to Joseph, Luke of Mary's consent. Men outside the Church, not believing either in angels or miracles, and seeing no particular point in virginity, judge both to be legends. Those Catholic scholars whose whole cast of mind would lead them to the same judgment are inhibited—partly by the continuing emphasis the Church has always laid on the Virgin Birth (we find Irenaeus writing of it within sixty years of John's death), partly by what the Virgin Mary has meant to themselves in their formative years. So they continue to believe in the Virgin Birth, "but not biologically." As we have noted, the phrase Virgin Birth is not in Scripture. Its phrases are, "I know not man," "Joseph knew her not." How does one fit a non-biological virginity into either?

Catholic moral theologians have been accused of casuistry, hair-splitting: but one reads Scripture scholars who can match them hair for hair. What emerges from too much of their study is a Christ unknown to the Evangelists. Once again, we remind ourselves that our present concern is with the Christ of the Gospels: only when we know him can we be aided by the scholars and not muddled.

2

In earlier chapters we spent a long time on the manhood of Jesus—on our growing awareness, as we meet him in the Gospels, that he was indeed man, but more than man: we used the phrase Man Plus. The phrase he himself used to signalize the same reality—we discussed it in Chapter IV—was "the Son of man." It is worth seeing the uses to which he puts it. Though "son of man" means man, Jesus rarely uses it for statements which might be made about any man. One remembers, of course, "the Son of man has nowhere to lay his head" and "the Son of man came eating and drinking." Each of these has its own way of being special. Otherwise Jesus reserves it for words and actions which fall outside the ordinary human sphere—it is definitely his interim way of saying Man Plus.

The first use recorded is when he is gathering his first Apostles, "You will see heaven opened, and the angels of God ascending and descending upon the Son of man" (John 1–51). That, perhaps you feel, is John—thirteen times he speaks of the Son of man in connection with ascent or descent; but in all the Gospels we find the Son of man linked with a glory to come. And here on earth he is shown with powers and privileges never asserted of man. The Son of man has power on earth to forgive sins, is Lord of the Sabbath, has come not to destroy, has descended from heaven, will come again with power to execute judgment, was foretold by Elias, sows the good seed in the field of the world, will be seen sitting at the right hand of God's power (all three Synoptics tell of this); unless men shall eat the flesh of the Son of man and drink his blood, they shall not have life in them (John 6); whoever shall be ashamed of him will not be acknowledged by him "when he comes in the glory of his Father with the angels" (Mark 8.38).

What did Jesus mean by the phrase? In Matthew's sixteenth chapter, note the two questions he puts to the Twelve—"Who do *men* say that the Son of man is?" "Who do *you* say that I am?" Peter answers the second —"the Christ, the Son of the Living God." But he does not cast any light on, nor do we ever hear him use, "Son of man."

In Chapter II it was noted that "Son of man" is only a way of saying man: so that the Son of man means The Man. In the opening chapters of Genesis, the first man is called "the Adam," which means "the man." Only after the sin does "the" vanish and Adam become simply the name by which he is referred to. It is at least not impossible that Jesus had this in mind. Jesus is "the Man" in whom redeemed humanity has its origin, as fallen humanity in Adam.

This would account for his continual use of the phrase in the foretelling of all the elements of his redemptive action. The Son of man is to be betrayed, is to be rejected by the leaders of the people, is to suffer, to be crucified, to rise again on the third day, to ascend to his heavenly Father. It was as man that he redeemed man, establishing a new humanity. Whatever his sonship of God meant it spared his manhood no effort, no agony.

There is a tendency to think that his followers invented the foretelling of the Passion after it happened. This goes with the swing of the pendulum. Jews and Christians alike used to think of prophecy only as foretelling. Now we are reminded that prophecy was essentially not foretelling but "forthtelling," speaking out. So foretelling is frowned out of existence altogether! The Baptist could not have called Christ the Lamb of God before "the Easter Experience," Christ could not have foretold the destruction of Jerusalem or his own death and resurrection. Why not? Because the critic does not believe in God's intervening in human affairs. But the God of both Testaments does indeed intervene. It would be odd if he gave the fore-runner no knowledge of the One he fore-ran, if he gave the Son he sent to redeem mankind no awareness of what the redeeming would involve.

That Paul had read the Gospel of Luke, his physician and close companion, we take for granted—probably Luke showed it to him in bits as he was writing it. In the first chapter Luke quotes the angel as saying to Mary of Nazareth: "You will conceive in your womb and bear a son . . . and he will be called the Son of the Most High. . . . The Holy Spirit will come upon you, and the power of the Most High will overshadow you; therefore the child to be born will be called holy, the Son of God." Would it be possible to utter that in a ten-word summary better than Paul uttered it to the Galatians (4.4): "God sent forth his son, born of a woman"? How much of the angel's message does that leave out? Jesus was "the Son of the Most High," a phrase unknown in the Old Testament, "the Son of God," another phrase equally unknown there (angels were called sons of God, so were Israelites, so were holders of certain offices—as king or judge). But "the Son of God" applied to an individual person was new—and most noticeably new when applied by the person himself!

We need not exaggerate "the"; but it cannot be for nothing that it is used always of Jesus, and only of Jesus. (Luke's genealogy of Jesus ends "the son of Enos, the son of Seth, the son of Adam, the son of God," but that is hardly to our point here.)

In the double sonship—of God, of Mary—lay the identity of Jesus. As the son of Mary, he was fully man. As the Son of God he was—what? As both—what? His identity matters to us vitally, because as Paul went on to tell the Galatians, in Jesus' sonship "we are redeemed." So we search for his identity. Had he to search for it himself? He calls himself "the Son of Man," he calls himself "the Son of God." Had he to grow into the knowledge that he was both? Had he to grow in understanding of what each meant in itself, of what the twofold reality meant in him?

I am forever being startled at the certainty with which men answer these questions as if they had had Jesus on their dissecting table or on their couch. I begin with the simple fact that in his utterance to men we find no hint of searching—always the impression of one in superb equilibrium, knowing what he was and what he had come to do. But when we meet him in the Gospels he was within a couple of years of his death, close to the fullness of the maturity that life on earth was to bring him.

What had the preparation been? We have spent some time on his unique relation to the Father—"No one knows the Son but the Father and no one knows the Father but the Son" (Matthew 11.27, Luke 10.22). How early did he know this? *How* did he know it? The Trinity cannot be known by any created mind without a revelation from God—as Jesus said in this, his first mention of it; prophets and kings had not known it, not Elias, therefore, not David. How did his own human mind know it? He does not tell us. No one else can.

Nor does he tell us how he knew that he himself, the carpenter, was the Son. As we have noted, there is a tendency among critics today to say that he learnt it for the first time after his baptism by John and the descent of the Holy Spirit in the form of a dove, when the voice from heaven proclaimed him as "beloved Son" (Matthew 3.17, Luke 3.22). Clearly Luke, for one, could not have thought so. He it is who gives Jesus' words about his Father in the Temple twenty years earlier.

That the whole sequel to the baptism must have affected Jesus profoundly is beyond doubt. We may speculate on it, realizing how much of it can be only speculation. Jesus was conceived and born God-man as we are conceived and born man. As we grow in manhood, he would have grown in God-manhood. By the mere fact of living, acting, reacting, we progress in discovery of what is actually involved in being a man, he of what is involved in being a God-man, a man with a relation to God the Father that no other man had. "Though he was Son," says Hebrews, "he learnt obedience by the things he suffered" (5.8).

There are critics who hold that Jesus *became* God when he heard the voice. But sonship is not like that. I am no more my own father's son now than I was at my conception. If I had never met him, or even heard of him, I should still be his son. I did meet him, lived with him, and in the process developed an awareness not only of him and of myself but of the meaning of fatherhood and sonship.

Jesus did of course learn about fatherhood from Joseph, who by accepting him became legally his father. That we can picture. But what he learnt about it from his heavenly Father we cannot picture. We can see only as much as he showed us in word and action. In the Gospels we can watch him *being* himself.

3

The Evangelists, as we noted in Chapter IV, did not "theologize" or philosophically analyze the God-man reality they experienced in Jesus. They recorded the experience of living with him and growing into awareness of the duality. In the rest of the New Testament, likewise, the fact was accepted and immense consequences drawn from it, but there was no effort to explore what we may call its structural reality, to draw a blueprint. But the exploration began very soon after—Irenaeus, for instance, knew Polycarp who had known John. It continues to this day.

Here I will summarize the main line, the longest continuous line, of theology on the Word-made-Flesh. It makes use of two key-words, Person and Nature. The orthodox Roman-Greek statement, defined at Chalcedon in 451, is that Christ was one Person, one self, one I, God the Son; in two natures—the nature of God which was his eternally, and the nature of man, spirit embodied or matter enspirited, conceived in time of a human mother. Jesus could say, "Whatever I see my Father doing, I do in like manner." He can say, "My soul is sorrowful even unto death." It seems like two different people speaking. Yet it is one same "I" which makes both statements, asserts limitless power, admits finitude. In other words, one person is acting and speaking on two levels, drawing on two sources of operation, two natures.

So runs the theology of the Incarnation, to me marvellously illuminating, yet still leaving a great area of darkness. Too many have expounded it as if the formula bathed everything in light. They know what divinity means, they know what humanity means, and where's the problem? One remembers Dickens' Count Smorltork who, having to write on Chinese metaphysics, looked up China in an encyclopedia, then looked up Metaphysics, and combined the information. In seminaries I have met Doctor Smorltork, in Chanceries Monsignor Smorltork (of whose theology the Doctor thinks little, especially if he has been the Doctor's pupil). A principal reason why this all-sufficing blueprint won't do is that the relation of person and nature even in our own very ordinary selves is so beyond our gaze. We know Descartes' effort to establish the "I"—"I think, therefore I am." But we are more certain of the I than of the thought. That I am I, I do not doubt. That I am a man I do not doubt. But whereas I can talk at length about my manhood, I can find nothing to say about my "I." About my occupations and interests, pains and pleasures, my hopes and plans I can talk, but the "I" who is occupied and interested, pained or pleased, hopeful, designing, somehow eludes my gaze. When I try to concentrate on "I" the film flickers and goes dark. In other words, I know what I am, but I don't know what I is.

If the relation of person and nature is so unclear in me, what must it be when the person is God? The human nature was real, not a shape God the Son had put on to facilitate his movements among men, as angels are shown doing in the Old Testament. What difference to its operation did the fact make that the Person whose humanity it was knew everything, could do everything? Was there some effect flowing into it from the divine person which does not flow into mine from me? We cannot know.

The *sinlessness* of which Jesus tells us—was this a virtue in him as man, or was it the intervention of the divine Person? Did the special relation to God which he constantly claimed mean that he literally could not sin? Or that his manhood was in such vital contact with God that sin was unthinkable? Or even that in temptation's fiercest moment there would be a veto from the Second Person of the Blessed Trinity? We do find him counting upon God's aid, praying for it as we do, but it is the aid of the Father, not of the Son—that is, he is not asking the aid of his own Godhead. We never find him taking advantage of that to get him out of the kind of difficulties that we have to cope with unaided by a divinity in the persons we are.

What about Christ's *knowledge?* There are elements in it of which we can be certain—in the sense that if they were not so he would not have been a man. His senses were genuine channels through which the outer world got through to his brain. His brain was a real brain, not simply there because he had to have a head (its absence would have excited comment) and heads have brains. The body played the same part in Christ's knowing as in ours. In him, as in us, the intellect took hold of what came to the brain and did its own work on it; he grew in knowledge and understanding by the ordinary ways of growing. Humanly speaking, there were things he knew one moment that he had not known the moment before. He learnt from experience and he learnt from being taught—the Galilee school teachers taught him the Scriptures, the Galilee fishermen taught him the Lake.

But if one accepts his unique union with God, it would be odd to dismiss the possibility that this might enter into his human knowing power, if only from the lived experience of being thus united. As an experience it could not have meant nothing to his human nature that it was God the Son's, as it makes a difference to us that our bodies are animated by a man and not an ape. What the experience was only he could tell us; and, as we have noted more than once, he doesn't.

We cannot assume that we have him whole and entire under our microscopes. Apart from the experience which was his of being united with the Second Person, there is the possibility of direct communication. The only certain guide to what a God-man could do or say is what the only God-man did do and say (a fact overlooked often enough by the avant-garde as by the last-ditcher). Studying the Christ of the Gospels, we do know that he had the power to read minds, the power to know what his friends and enemies would do, to know what God planned for him. He tells us that he is doing what the Father has given him to do. So that in addition to the ways of knowledge he shared with all men, there were the ways of knowledge he shared with the prophets: whatever knowledge he needed for the work God had sent him to do, God saw to it that he had.

Did he know about Einstein's relativity? Improbable, one feels; it had no obvious connection with his mission. But how did he learn, when did he learn, about his own relation to God, about his relation to the whole human race, about the passion he must suffer and the death he must die? Today's mood is to shy away from anything in him which cannot be explained solely in terms of his manhood undiluted by divinity—as if the divine could be a dilution. One feels that critics feel that the manhood could preserve its integrity only by holding the divinity at arm's length, forcing it to keep its distance.

Which brings us to one other question over which we cannot fail to wonder. What did it mean to God the Son that he should be the person, the self, in a human nature? Whatever the duties of person to nature, this was one Person who could bring infinite love to them. Human nature—in us as in Christ—is a cry to God. The person we are utters it, weakly or strongly. God the Son would have been failing his manhood if he had not uttered its adoration, thanksgiving, petition—not contrition, or course. But he would not merely *utter* the nature, dutifully rubber-stamping with his "I" whatever the manhood said or felt. The Person was operative within the nature, its actions were his as well as its.

The human anguish did not mean nothing to him personally, he was not merely doing his duty to his nature by lending its anguish such concurrence as it would have been entitled to expect if the person had been human like itself. That the divine Person, in some way inconceivable to us, suffered in the humanity Paul tells us: "God did not spare his own Son" (Romans 8.32). On such things it is human to speculate, and we all do. But speculation, however learned, is not knowledge. The ultimate authority on Christ must always be Christ.

The analyzing of what he has given us falls to the theologians and the exegetes. Orthodox and far out, there is something to be gained from all of them. They have done a splendid work, but never complete or in this life completable. I have called John's "The Word was God . . . and the Word became flesh" a milestone. So was Augustine's insight that the Holy Spirit is produced by the love of Father and Son. So was the One Person in two Natures of Chalcedon. Men advance in the knowledge of God by prayer and thought, by the study of His creation, by living as He has willed; they advance in the knowledge of men by a score of roads. We are waiting, patiently or impatiently according to our temperament, for a new Chalcedon to synthesize all this into a profounder statement on the God-man. When it comes, it will still be a milestone. For full knowledge we must wait till we see Him. As John tells us in his First Epistle, "When he appears we shall be like him, for we shall see him as he is."

POSTSCRIPT: *Thinking Aloud on the Fourth Gospel*

The teaching on Father, Son and Holy Spirit, and on the entry of the Son into the human race, John illuminates but does not originate. It would be hard to isolate any element in either doctrine that is solely his. But he

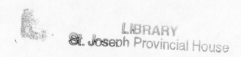

does illuminate, does enrich. Was it simply his own re-flection, through thirty years more, on the Jesus who loved him best of all his followers and entrusted his mother to him? Was it perhaps a development in the whole Church during that same thirty-year period, half the Church's life? Certainly no hint has reached us that his Gospel caused the surprise that it causes now, seemed as original then as it seems now. Indeed, had John given his Gospel as fruit either of his own reflec-tion or the Church's, it would be less argued about today. What bothers critics are the words he puts into Jesus' mouth, words reported by no other, at Capharnaum after the feeding of the five thousand, in the Temple, at the Last Supper.

I do not know the answer. I merely think aloud about the problem. The argument that John could not have remembered such long speeches after sixty years is not to the point. Over the centuries visitors to the Middle East have remarked on the incredible memories there. In any event he might indeed have written them down at once! He and the others might have talked them over among themselves again and again through the years in which the new Church was not ready for them, years in which even they themselves had not penetrated them deeply.

Reading the words, I feel that they could only have their source in Jesus himself—who else has ever talked like that? They seem to me as evidently his as the Ser-mon on the Mount. Subjective? Of course. But not more so than the feeling of so many readers that the Bible is God's inspired word. If they are from Jesus, when did he utter them? We know that chronology meant less to the Evangelists than to us. They would put an event or an utterance not necessarily when it happened or was said but along with things said or done at another time—logical fitness, not chronological. We know it is so with the Sermon on the Mount. There are those who think that the conferring of the primacy on Peter—"I will give you the keys of the kingdom of heaven"—came after the Resurrection, and was placed by Matthew where we find it because of its logical connection with Peter's "Thou art the Christ, the Son of the living God." There is a kind of fascination in reading Christ's long discourses at the Last Supper in John's chapters 14–17, trying to see which of them would have come more aptly in the forty days between Resurrection and Ascension. But I am not asserting any of this.

Chapter XII

Priest of a Cosmic Sacrifice

Jesus was crucified by Roman soldiers at the command of a Roman official, Pontius Pilate. That is one fact about him which no one denies. Even for those who are constitutionally disinclined to believe a word of the Gospels, there is the pagan historian Tacitus who tells it in his Annals: he would not have dreamed of stating it on any but official Roman authority—certainly not to oblige Christian apologists (he described the Christians martyred under Nero as "scum" or "dregs").

From the Gospels we learn two further things, one of which would have amused Tacitus; the other he would not have believed. The first is that Pilate ordered the crucifixion reluctantly, not from any feeling either for Jesus or justice, but from sheer dislike of having his hand forced by the Jewish High Priest. The second is that Christ not only knew a couple of years earlier the death he was to die, but chose to suffer it. He saw it indeed as the purpose of his existence. Think closely on John 12.27. Jesus' soul was troubled; should he ask his Father to save him from this hour? "No," he answered himself, "it was for this purpose that I came to this hour."

We have already seen how the death that awaited him shadowed the road on which he had set his feet. He lived in the horror of it and the fear of it, but did not flinch from it. He continued the challenge to the Establishment which made it certain that the Establishment would torture and slay him.

Observe that he did not challenge the authority of the Roman masters of his country. It was the religious Establishment that felt him as a mortal threat—the Pharisees to their spiritual leadership, the Sadducees to the modus vivendi with the Romans under which they lived and grew fat. From the very beginning of the twenty-six months of Jesus' teaching and miracle-working, he was in conflict with scribes and Pharisees—bad men concerned for their own spiritual prestige and financial well-being, good men who saw him as denying beliefs and practices which seemed to them at the heart of Israel's religion.

The conflict with both sorts of Pharisees was continuous. But in the end it was the Sadducees who forced Pilate to crucify him. John tells us (11.46) that the raising to life of Lazarus brought them into action. A miracle so spectacular, within a mile or two of the capital, was certain to cause vast throngs of excited people, always for the Romans a danger signal. It did in fact cause the Palm Sunday demonstrations. The Roman machine might take over completely, dispensing with the Sadducee High Priests (who were their appointees). So Jesus must be stopped. In the revealing phrase of Caiphas, "it is expedient *for you* that one man should die for the people" the italics are mine, but mentally they belong to Caiphas—"the people" for whom one man must die meant themselves, the privileged, the ones who mattered.

There were two reasons why the Romans had to be used for the slaying. One was that they could legally inflict the death penalty. The other was that only the Romans had a grip strong enough to enable them to get away with murder—this particular murder especially. Caiphas and the rest realized that they must do it "by stealth," and not on the day of the Feast, "lest there should be an uproar among the people" (Matthew 26.5).

John comments that Caiphas said more than he meant or said, God using him as High Priest to "prophesy that Jesus should die not only for the Jewish nation, but to gather into one the children of God who are scattered abroad." Throughout the story we see evil men, Caiphas and Annas, Judas, Pilate (to say nothing of Satan) acting solely for their own purposes and accomplishing Christ's.

Judas, for example. Matthew (26.24), Mark and Luke too, tell how Jesus, after answering that one of the Twelve would betray him, continued that the Son of Man would go on the way ordained for him (as foretold in Scripture)—but that it would have been better for the betrayer if he had never been born.

Satan tempted, Judas took his thirty pieces of silver, High Priests schemed, Pilate compromised—and the upshot was the world's redemption. But what had the crucifixion of the Galilean carpenter to do with the world's redemption? That that was the point of it, Jesus makes clear again and again. But what does it mean? He suffered and died heroically, but how does his heroism help us? How does his rising from the dead?

I

> Tell me the old old story . . .
> of Jesus and his love

The lines are from a Wesleyan hymn I loved as a small boy. In those dear dead distant days, that a belief was old was a point in its favor, an extra splendor, it had stood the test of ages. Today it is a prima facie reason for rejecting it out of hand. Speaking of Christ's Passion and Death to outdoor crowds, I have had hecklers sing back at me "Tell me the old old story"—making a taunt of what once was a splendor. Even convinced Catholics have constantly to remind themselves that a belief is not proved wrong because they have held it all their lives.

All the same, the oldness of this particular story carries a danger with it. The hymn goes on:

> Tell me the story often
> That I may take it in
> That wonderful Redemption
> God's remedy for sin.

We have indeed been told the story often: so often that it has lost its freshness. We have heard the same incidents, in the same order, almost in the same words, told by preachers who had heard it in the same admirable form from men before them who had heard it. . . . I have sometimes felt during such a sermon how reviving it would be if a handful of hecklers would stand up in the church and sing "Tell me the old old story." We can still, of course, react to the sermon emotionally, though the main emotion may be nostalgia for our childhood in the Faith. But our minds may not be in action at all. We "take it in," but not dynamically; its meaning does not grow deeper, and newer at each new depth.

What did the Passion and Death mean to Jesus Christ himself? "This is my body which is broken for you," he said at the Last Supper. "This is the chalice of my blood which is to be shed for you." But what do the words "for you" mean? With one sentence, which does not figure in the form in which the telling of the story has crystallized, he gives us the key.

We find it in Luke's account of the Supper (22.37). Jesus spoke of a scripture still to be fulfilled in him— namely, "He was reckoned with the transgressors," a quotation from Isaiah (53.12). He repeated "What is written about me is having its fulfillment." So, in this grim great moment he points us back to chapter 53 of Isaiah. Anyone who has not read it recently would be wise to read it now. "Wise" is putting it mildly. Not to study it closely is to refuse the key Jesus offers as to the meaning *to himself* of what he did and suffered between leaving the Supper room on the Thursday night and dying on the next afternoon.

The sentence Jesus quotes comes in the last verse of the chapter—"He poured out his soul to death and was numbered among the transgressors: yet he bore the sin of many and made intercession for the guilty." The sentence before speaks of "the Righteous One, my servant; he shall make many to be accounted righteous, bearing their iniquities." And the sentence before that has "he shall make himself an offering for sin"—offering, we remember, was the decisive part of sacrifice: and a sin-offering meant a victim slain. But only the priest could make the offering. Verses 4 and 5 summarize the whole chapter: he had the air of one "stricken, smitten by God and afflicted. But he was wounded for our transgressions, he was bruised for our iniquities. Upon him was the chastisement that made us whole, and with his scourging we are healed."

Was Isaiah consciously writing of one man who should die for the redemption of all? To many Jews it seems that he was not writing of one particular Jew still to come, but of the whole people, Israel. Jews apart, there is the present refusal to believe that any prophecy actually foretells. Readers of that mind see Isaiah drawing the picture of the just man through the ages suffering for justice' sake. And indeed what he has drawn is a kind of pattern exemplified in all who have thus suffered, Gentiles and Jews alike. "He was led like a lamb to the slaughter, like a sheep before his shearers he opened not his mouth." That would fit others, the Mohammedan Al Hallaj for example, slain by the leaders of his own people.

Exemplified, yes, but fulfilled only once. There is too much in the chapter which could fit none but Jesus of Nazareth. "His birth is beyond our knowing" does not mean only that we happen to lack information about his parentage, as about Melchizedek's: "He who never did wrong" hardly applies to Israel. "All we like sheep have gone astray, and the Lord has laid on him the iniquity of us all"—with what other man could the whole human race be so identified that his death could be thus vastly redemptive? That Isaiah's prophecy was now fulfilled, Jesus clearly said. We must study what happened, in Gethsemane and at the trial and on Calvary, in the awareness that Jesus saw himself as being wounded for our transgressions, scourged for our healing, slain for our redeeming—all this by God's will and his own choice.

What one individual present at the Last Supper

made of the Isaiah chapter we find in Peter's First Epistle (2.22–25). He sums it up superbly in the sentence "on
the cross his own body bore"—i.e., took the weight of—
"our sins." If Jesus had not thus directed the Apostles to
Isaiah, we and even Peter would hardly have known
that it was the weight of our sins which made Gethsemane's deepest agony for him, and its special problem
for us.

For there *is* a special problem. Up to Gethsemane
Jesus lived indeed in the shadow of the suffering which
awaited him, but was wholly in control of himself and
of every situation. Within a few days of his death he
could goad his executioners with "The harlots shall enter the kingdom of heaven before you." John indeed
shows him feeling the horror of "the hour" as it drew
near but not asking his Father to save him from it since
it was for this very hour that he had come (12.27). But in
Gethsemane, though still in total submission to God's
will, he *does* ask his Father, "If it be your will, let this
cup pass from me."

It is the first even momentary hesitation we have
seen in him, and it puzzles us. Was he simply asking to
be spared the suffering and death? But he had called
this "Satanic" when Peter had urged it on him a while
before. Not only that. He had more than once warned
the Apostles that these very things were certain to happen. We have just heard him saying that it was for this
hour that he had come. At the Last Supper, so brief a
while before, he had ritually and sacramentally committed himself to death.

Clearly a new element had entered into the suffering,
and from Isaiah we know what it was. He had accepted
to take upon himself the sin of mankind, "he bore the

sin of many," says Isaiah, "and made intercession for the guilty." This, not death alone, was the "cup he was to drink," the cup he for a moment wished his Father would take away from him. He had known about the cup, of course. When James and John asked for the places on his right hand and his left in the kingdom (Matthew 20.22), he put them the test question "Can you drink the cup that I am to drink?" Why yes, they answered him. They had no notion how bitter the cup might be. But at that time neither had he!

He had agreed to accept such an identification with the race of men that their sins could become his burden —not the guilt of them, which goes only with the sinning, but the weight of the guilt—the sorrow for all the obedience refused, for repentance unfelt, for so measureless an ocean of callousness towards God and man. In Gethsemane the identification with sinful men was made—"he who knew no sin became sin for us," says Paul (2 Corinthians 5.21).

"On the cross," we have just heard Peter say, "his body took the weight of our sins." In the Garden his whole being took that weight. There is mystery here. We are at the central point of Christ's uniqueness. We have no experience to give us a notion of what such an identification of one man with all men might be in its actuality. But we catch a glimpse of what it meant psychologically and emotionally. "He grew fearful," says Peter through Mark. "My soul is sorrowful even unto death," he cried (Mark 14.36). The cup was now at his lips. He had known theoretically what it was to be. But the reality was beyond all theorizing. It is after telling of his agony—"prayers and supplications and loud cries and tears"—that Hebrews says, "Though he was son, he learned obedience by the things he suffered.

. . . And he is the means of salvation to all who obey him." From Christ's redemption no one is excluded.

But Paul speaks to the Ephesians (1.10) of a wider range: "It was God's loving design, centered in Christ, to give history its fulfilment by resuming everything in him, all that is in heaven, all that is on earth, summed up in him." As Vatican II phrases it: "Christ's redemptive work involves the renewal of the whole temporal order."

2

When we hear that splendid hymn "Were you there when they crucified my Lord?" the reaction of most of us is that we were! Almost, anyway. What with Gospel reading, sermons, the Holy Week liturgy, the Sorrowful Mysteries of the Rosary, the Stations of the Cross, great paintings, oratorios—the whole event is vivid in our minds as no other past event is. The trouble is that the actual Gospel account can be overlaid by so much splendor.

Take one example. Nothing in all the Liturgy is more dramatic than the Reproaches on Good Friday—a chanting of the great things God has done for the Jews, each one contrasted with what they did to the God-Man. It is intensely moving as meditation after the event, but it is no part of what happened. From end to end of the Suffering and Death there was not a word of reproach from Jesus. It was of the essence of what he had come to do that there should not be. We must make the vast effort to strip our minds of all that we have heard said and sung or seen depicted, and submit ourselves to the Gospel account.

The effort will indeed be vast, so cluttered are our

minds with ideas true, half-true, false. And when we have made the effort, there is another danger. We can hardly help "identifying" with Jesus, thinking and feeling with him. It is right that we should. But this experience is strictly personal. It cannot but reflect what our own thoughts and feelings would have been if we had been he! But no man can be any other man, least of all this Other. Published reflections on the Passion only occasionally harmonize with our own, we can even find them repellent—especially if they be of the lush and oratorical sort. Lush and oratorical he was not. (In my own private opinion it would have been better for the world if all the born orators had been born dead.) At any rate I shall not bother you with any of my own insights, if that be the word for them, into the depth of Jesus' soul. I shall stay with what he said and did.

In the whole Gospel account, what looms towering is the untroubled rationality of his every word. The secret lies in chapter 53 of Isaiah, which he had told them at the Last Supper was in process of fulfilment, and which proves to have been the scenario of the drama of mankind's redemption. The "scripture" he quotes as still to be fulfilled (Luke 22.37), we remind ourselves, is in the last verse of the chapter—"He poured out his soul to death and was numbered among the transgressors: yet he bore the sin of many and made intercession for the guilty."

A few lines before, we read "He shall make himself an offering for sin." It is a stunning sentence. Offering was the decisive part of sacrifice: sin-offerings called for the slaying of the victim, but while the slaying might be done by others (the Temple servants, for instance), only the priest could make the offering. So that Isaiah is speaking of a sacrifice in which Priest and Victim were one person. In our thinking we tend to concentrate on Christ as victim, but his torturing and slaying was the work of his enemies. Their slaying him would have made him a martyr but not a sacrificial victim. Only his own offering did that.

In the sacrifices of the Old Testament, the victim had no contribution to make: its presence was needed and its death, but it did not "contribute" either: it was brought there and slain there: it was purely passive. Isaiah writes of "the lamb that is led to the slaughter, a sheep that opened not its mouth." So with Jesus. As victim he says nothing. For the victim to have complained, to have reproached his slayers, would have been wholly outside the symmetry of the sacrifice. Unless we see him as a Priest, we have missed the point of Calvary. As his slayers did.

From the moment of his arrest, everything Jesus said was the utterance of a man wholly in his own control, one who knew exactly what he was doing, where he was going. And this continued almost to the moment of his death. The fragmented dialogue between him and "the high priests and elders and scribes," the hard core of his enemies, reads as if a civilized man were answering primitives: for those highly civilized men had been stripped down by rage to an elemental baseness. And of course they did not know that they were taking part in the ritual of a cosmic sacrifice. How could they?

Chapter XIII

Death Takes Jesus but Cannot Hold Him

I

We have seen the long moment of unsureness in Gethsemane. In his fear and misery (Mark 14.32) Jesus had said to Peter, James and John, "My soul is very sorrowful, even to death." He asked them to hold off sleep and pray: their faith in him was going to be tested as never before, and he warned them "the spirit is willing, but the flesh is weak." But sleep they did, right through his Agony, as the same three had slept through his Transfiguration.

From the Garden Jesus could have seen the Temple guard with their "lances and torches and weapons," as they came out from the city gate on the other side of that very narrow valley. The crisis was over. He was himself again, and at a new level of serenity. He showed no anger at the Apostles who had slept, only a sad "Couldn't you stay awake with me for an hour?" To the guards he said, "Why the swords and clubs? I was within your reach as I sat teaching in the Temple day after day, and you never laid a hand on me."

Judas had kissed him to show the guards which one they were to arrest—the most famous, but not the first and not the last, betrayal with a kiss. The Greek word means an affectionate kiss, no mere brushing with the lips. If this strikes you as strange, think what the ferment must have been in Judas' mind: after all, he was to commit suicide next day. We note that the kind of violence is gone from Jesus which once caused him to call Judas a devil. Knowing of the treachery, he could still say, "Friend, what have you come for?" As we have noted, it is the only time we hear him address anyone as "friend."

So we come to the most farcical episode in all Scripture, one of the few happenings told in all four Gospels. Peter lashed out with his sword, and cut off the ear of a slave of the High Priest. Why the ear? Why the slave? If he had to smite someone, why not one of the guards? Indeed, why not Judas?

We can speculate as to what Peter thought he was doing. After all, Christ had told the Apostles to buy a sword and had agreed to their bringing two (Luke 22.33): to this day we don't know what he meant by it. Jesus restored the ear, his last recorded miracle of healing, and ordered Peter to sheathe his sword, for "all those who take up the sword will perish by the sword." The whole episode leaves one marvelling at those of Peter's successors who thought to serve their Master with the sword.

Peter, about to flee away with the rest (so soon after their first Eucharist!), had had his last spurt of courage: before the night was out, he was to deny that he knew Christ—one of his denials being made to a relative of the man whose ear he had sliced off. Jesus had had his last flicker of uncertainty, when he cried out to his Father for release from the anguish of the cup which was being pressed to his lips. In his last words on the Peter farce, he dismissed all that finally (John 18.11): "Shall I not drink the cup which my Father has given me?"

2

"The soldiers and their captain and the officers of the Jews" pinioned Jesus and took him first to the house of Annas, formerly High Priest by Roman appointment. To Annas' questioning, Jesus said: "Why ask me? Ask those who have heard me." An officer, accustomed to servility in prisoners, struck him. Again he was quietly reasonable: "If I have said anything I shouldn't, show where I'm wrong. If I have not, what is the point of striking me?" Annas sent him on, still pinioned, to the reigning High Priest, his daughter's husband Caiphas.

In these opening confrontations with leaders of the Sanhedrin, as at Pilate's tribunal and in Herod's palace, Jesus stays master of himself through a stream of barbarities—blows and spitting and mockeries, lashes and a crown of thorns. He makes no complaint, after this first blow no comment even. He answers those legally entitled to question him but no one else.

The Evangelists do not luxuriate in the horrors. We know, for example, what a Roman scourging was: merely reading the details can turn the stomach. But we do not read them in the Gospels. We are simply told that Pilate had him scourged, and then presented the scourged man to the crowd as a reason against bothering to go on with the crucifixion. His "Ecce homo" could only have meant "Look at him now." Jesus must have been blood-bathed, but none of them mention blood till he is dead. They do not utter their own feelings, as he does not utter his. He complained of nothing, blamed no one, judged no one, was wholly judged.

Everyone must read the four accounts for himself—chapters 21 and 22 of Matthew, 14 and 15 of Mark, 22 and 23 of Luke, 18 and 19 of John. I can only record my own impression—that he allowed none of the tortures he suffered as Victim to disturb his central concentration on what he was doing as Priest, for the redemption of the whole human race.

When we hear the hymn "Were you there when they crucified my Lord?" we feel a stirring of kinship with Our Lady and Mary Magdalen, with Mary of Cleophas and Salome the mother of James and John, possibly even with Simon of Cyrene and the thief who repented. But it might occasionally be profitable to consider others who could have said "yes" to the hymn's question. Have we any kinship with the bystanders who mocked him, with the chief priests and scribes who led the mockery, with the soldiers who nailed him to the cross and threw dice for his clothes, with Peter who stayed away brooding (surely) over his denials, with Pilate the official provider of the spectacle? Happy we if we can think of any of them with no twinge of discomfort about our own selves.

Between his arrest and his appearance before the pagan Roman governor, Jesus had two confrontations with his own people. The first was late at night before Annas and Caiphas, the second at sunrise before the Sanhedrin, the high court of Israel. Neither was a trial. The first was to assemble evidence against him, the second to persuade the Sanhedrin that he deserved to be sent for trial by Pontius Pilate.

What I have called the hard core of those who were determined on his death were in vigorous action—chief priests (Sadducees), scribes (mostly Pharisees), and elders. We have already met them heckling Christ about his authority to teach and not coming very well out of it (Mark 11.27). We are to meet them again. They were at the night meeting, at Pilate's tribunal, in Herod's house, on Calvary.

The enemies of Jesus included men of every degree of piety and every degree of worldliness (like ourselves). But they did sincerely believe in the God of Israel and they were convinced that Jesus was a blasphemer, an enemy of God. Caiphas was wholly sincere when he said, "I adjure you by the living God, tell us if you are the Christ the Son of God." At Caesarea Philippi Jesus had asked the Twelve, "Who do men say I am?"; then "Who do you say I am?" Peter had answered, "You are the Christ, the Son of the living God." Now Caiphas put the same question to Jesus himself—"Who do *you* say you are?" And his question reproduces Peter's answer so closely that one feels he must have been told of it, by Judas perhaps. However that may be, he knew, as the Twelve knew and so many of us have forgotten, that the key question was "Who *is* Jesus?"

It is the second time we have heard Caiphas' question. In the Portico of Solomon his hearers had challenged him. "How long will you keep us in suspense? If you are the Christ, tell us plainly." And he had told them, but not plainly. We may wonder if his answer to Caiphas too lacked plainness. What he said was "You say that I am." He was to answer Pilate's question "Are you the king of the Jews?" in the same way (Matthew 27.11). One has read that it was a Jewish way of saying yes, and indeed Mark writes Jesus' answer simply as "I am." The wording is certainly curious, for Caiphas had definitely not made the one statement or Pilate the other. It may have been a way of saying that their lips had uttered phrases of majesty, if only as questions. Certainly Jesus was not evading a straight answer. He went on, "Hereafter you will see the Son of man seated at the right hand of Power, and coming on the clouds of heaven."

Caiphas saw no evasion. For him it was the admission of blasphemy he needed to convince the Sanhedrin, indeed to convince himself. Jesus had warned his followers that by slaying them men would believe they were serving God. This was the case of himself and Caiphas. The High Priest had wanted to be rid of Jesus for the worldliest of reasons, namely that Jesus was a threat to his own position. Now he could feel that the execution would serve not only his own interests but God's. All believers know the situation—the thing we want to do yet are dubious about, till we have convinced ourselves that it is what God would certainly want of us. It is the tragedy, the tragi-comedy, of the human conscience.

From what we know of Caiphas he had no very sensitive conscience. But upon this matter his conscience was unshadowed. What Jesus had said meant to Caiphas what it had meant to the Jews by the Sheep Gate —that in "calling God his Father he was making himself equal with God" (John 4.18). The rending of his garments—a few inches from the neck down—was a ritual act. His horror was his own.

But it is another element in the tragi-comedy of conscience that men sure of the righteousness of their purpose will use the crookedest means to achieve it. It is an abiding danger for religious men to think that Omniscience can be served by falsehood, Omnipotence by trickery. So now, to Caesar's representatives who were to be manipulated into executing him, they accused Jesus of usurping not God's rights, but Caesar's.

3

The High Priest and the rest, convinced that Jesus deserved death as a blasphemer, handed him over to the Roman governor, Pontius Pilate. There may have been other occasions, but they do not leap to mind, on which Israel's religious leaders had officially called upon the Gentile conqueror to put one of their own people to death on a religious charge. The confrontation of Christ and Pilate will tell us more about Christ and the world and ourselves than anything in the Gospels. To get the fullest picture, it is best to study it in a Harmony—the Gospels set out in parallel columns, one Gospel providing elements that another lacks.

As we have observed, Caiphas asked to have Jesus slain not for blasphemy against God but for treason against Caesar—for "perverting the nation, forbidding the payment of tribute to Caesar, saying that he himself is Christ a king." The first question Pilate asks Jesus in all four accounts—"Are you the king of the Jews?"—shows sufficiently the line they had already taken with him.

John, who knew a relative of the High Priest and had been at the first confrontation, could not have been absent from this. He records Jesus' answer (John 18.36): "My kingship is not of this world. If it were, my servants would be fighting. No, my kingship is not from the world." "So you *are* a king?" said Pilate. "You say that I am a king. For this I was born, for this I have come into the world, to bear witness to the truth. Every one who is of the truth hears my voice."

Carefully studied, this answer brings us to the essence of Christ's mission and therefore of our part in it. It settled the matter for Pilate too, but differently. "What is truth?" he asked—as much as to say, "Truth! Is that all?" The Middle East was one endless tangle of philosophies and prophecies, mysticisms and occultisms. The Roman civil service treated them all with contemptuous tolerance. They were harmless, no threat to Rome's rule, no concern therefore of Pilate's. The Jews clearly had reasons of their own for so passionately wanting this particular fanatic dead. But their evidence left Pilate unconvinced.

As a Roman magistrate his whole training was for legality, where Rome's interests or his own were not involved. He made two efforts to get rid of the problem —first by sending Jesus on to Herod who was visiting Jerusalem, then by suggesting that he be chosen as the prisoner to be freed in honor of Passover. But Herod sent him back, and the Jews gathered in the street by Pilate's tribunal shouted for Barabbas to be released and Jesus to be crucified.

So the problem was back with Pilate. Why did he make such a fight to save a carpenter from Galilee? He said he could find no fault in him, but there is nothing in his bloodstained career to suggest that that would have mattered very much. Verses 7–12 of John 19 suggest that Pilate was half under the spell of Jesus' mystery. He could not be dismissed as simply one more fanatic, so serenely rational was everything he said—when, that is, he chose to say anything at all.

For his silence was troubling. "Have you no word for me?" Pilate almost pleaded with the prisoner. "Don't you realize that I have the power to crucify you or release you?" The answer that came from the tortured wreck in front of him was "You would have no power over me at all, if it had not been given you from above. Therefore the man who gave me up to you is more guilty yet." So the prisoner was declaring his judge guilty! Why was he not handed over to the torturers? There is the hint of an answer in verses 7–8. The Jewish leaders told Pilate for the first time that Jesus "pretended to be the son of God." The phrase itself meant nothing to Pilate, all the gods he knew about had sons, lots of them. Yet "he was more afraid than ever"—afraid the prisoner might really be a god, perhaps. And there was the message sent to him by his wife of which Matthew tells: "The man is innocent. Leave him alone. I dreamed today that I suffered much on his account."

At this point his enemies played their trump card. "If you release him, you are no friend of Caesar's." The threat of reporting Pilate to Caesar had been there from the beginning. Now it was uttered. Three times before they had reported him to the Emperor Tiberius, and twice the decision had gone humiliatingly against him. He did not yet know that his career was to be ended a few years after by a report sent to Caesar of a massacre of his in Samaria. But he was in mortal panic—his powerful patron, the Jew-hating Sejanus, either had just been, or was soon to be, executed by Tiberius.

The prisoner's possible divinity could not weigh with

him against Tiberius' terrifying certainty. So he handed Jesus over for crucifixion, creating a metaphor which guaranteed his immortality by literally washing his hands to show himself innocent of the slaying of an innocent man!

4

I have been present, as speaker or listener, at thousands of religious meetings and have heard scores of thousands of objections. Only a handful stay clear in my head, one clearer than the rest. "Christ on the cross," said the objector, "was unnecessarily melodramatic. He made too much fuss." The speaker was so startled that all he could say was "If ever you come to be crucified, I hope you will set us all an example of quiet good taste."

From the arrest in the Garden to the moment of death, fuss was precisely what Jesus did not make, the drama he was living through was a whole solar system away from melodrama. And once again we note that the Evangelists made no effort to melodramatize or even dramatize it. The way to Calvary gets one verse each from Matthew, Mark and John. Luke adds the detail of the weeping women who—along with two criminals—walked the way with him: to the women Jesus said: "Do not weep for me, but for yourselves and your children. The days are coming when they will say, 'Blessed are the barren, the wombs that never bore, the breasts that never suckled.'"

Nor was there any melodrama on Calvary. Mostly it was silence. The hard-core enemies, "chief priests and scribes and elders," were clearly maddened by their failure to draw one word from him. He had made no answer to their accusations before Caiphas, before

Herod, before Pilate. Now that he was nailed to the cross they, and the passers-by with them, taunted him with the failure of his kingship, the futility of his claim to sonship of God.

One feels that their taunts barely reached him. He was offering the supreme sacrifice to his Father, redeeming the human race, them included. The Gospels record his speaking seven times (we do not know in what order)—three times about others, three times about himself, once about the completion of his work. The seven make a collection of utterances wholly comparable, in all save length, with the Sermon on the Mount. In the Sermon he had preached, on the Cross he lived what he preached.

"Father, forgive them, for they do not know what it is they are doing" (Luke 25.34), taken with his "the spirit is willing but the flesh is weak," constitutes a kind of Magna Carta for ourselves and all the sinners that ever have been or will be—the one allowing for inadequacy in the intellect, the other in the will. It is Luke also who tells of the two criminals. They had joined in the taunting from their crosses on each side of his, but one of them had a deathbed conversion more astonishing than any other, considering the nature of the "bed" and the present condition of the One to whom he said, "Remember me when you come into your kingdom." To him Jesus said, "Today you will be with me in paradise."

The third of these words about others is told us by John, "the disciple whom Jesus loved"—how Jesus "said to his Mother, 'Woman, this is your son,'" and to the disciple, "This is your Mother"—and from that hour the disciple took her into his own keeping.

Of the three things Jesus said about himself, one has

gripped the minds of believers and unbelievers. Matthew and Mark both record it: "My God, my God, why hast thou forsaken me?" We find the question at once towering and shattering. That it is a cry of desolation everyone feels instantly, because everyone has at some time cried it for himself. No one needs to wait for it in the Gospels to have felt forsaken and to have challenged God with Why? Many a reader who has not been drawn to the Jesus of preaching and parable and miracle has felt kinship with him on first hearing those words.

But in any two of us the experience is not identical, neither the desolation nor its intensity. What did they mean in him? Part of the effect on ourselves results from coming on the words *by* themselves, as if they were forged in the fire of Jesus' anguish. But they were a quotation, the four-word opening phrase of Psalm 22 (21), *Eloi, Eloi, lama sabactani.*

It was customary then, among Christians it still is, to bring a whole psalm into consideration by saying its opening word or words. So we speak of the *Miserere,* the *De Profundis.* These happen to be splendid words, but without the psalm they introduce they could be made to mean anything. Because in their own power the words "My God, my God, why hast thou forsaken me?" can mean a desolation we have known ourselves, we may feel we need look no further. But what do they mean in the psalm? Do read it.

At the Last Supper Jesus referred his listeners to Isaiah 53 for light upon the things that were to be done to him. On Calvary he referred them to Psalm 22 (21) for light upon what was being done to him before their gaze. Each was at once a scenario and a commentary, the second an astonishingly detailed scenario. When

Jesus uttered the psalm's opening words, "My God, my God, why hast thou forsaken me?" he would have brought the whole psalm to the mind of all Jews present —to their mind, to their very eyes. "I am a worm and no man, scorned by men—They have pierced my hands and my feet, I can count all my bones—They stare and gloat over me, they divide my garments among them, and for my raiment they cast lots." That other cry from the Cross, "I thirst," was there too—"Parched is my throat like clay in the baking, and my tongue cleaves to my jaws, thou dost lay me in the dust of death." The high priests and scribes and elders must have had at least a moment of shock to meet themselves: "All who see me mock at me, mouthing out their scorn, saying 'He trusted his cause to the Lord, let the Lord rescue him, for he delights in him!' "

To whom are all these things happening? To the Psalmist? To Israel? To One who is to come? Jesus, mentioning it now, relates it all to himself. When he said, "My God, my God, why hast thou forsaken me?" "me" clearly means himself. But what does the whole phrase mean in the psalm? Not that God has withdrawn His presence, but His aid—"Why art thou so far from *helping* me?" God is letting his enemies, "a company of evildoers who encircle me," have their appalling way with him. Why does God not intervene? Thus far the psalm is a summary of the book of Job.

Was Jesus crying his own desolation as Job was? Was he at least questioning God as Job did? Each will decide this for himself out of the personality his own experience of life has shaped in him. I can only say how it seems to me. One fact is not in dispute: the whole psalm is not of desolation. Its second half is wholly a cry of confidence in God more positive than any Job shows. The Lord "has not despised or abhorred the affliction of the afflicted; and he has not hid his face from him, but has heard, when he cried to him." And it concludes: "Men shall tell of the Lord to the coming generation, and proclaim his deliverance to a people yet unborn, that he has wrought it." If he was questioning God, he answers his own questions.

But was he? All the rest that we hear from his lips on Calvary suggests that he was not. He had given his mother a new son, had promised paradise to the repentant thief, had asked his Father to forgive his own unrepentant slayers. The second and third were obviously redemptive actions fitting in with the sacrifice he was offering for mankind's redemption. So was the first, the Church thinks (I too, for that matter). And he was about to yield up his spirit to the Psalmist's God and his own: "Into thy hands I commit my spirit"—that is from verse 5 of Psalm 30: the verse continues—"thou hast redeemed me, O Lord, faithful god . . . because thou hast seen my affliction . . . and hast not delivered me into the hand of the enemy" (6, 7).

Apart from what else he said on the Cross, I find it hard to think that, having accepted without a murmur all the agony of his Victim state to the point of achievement, he should choose this ultimate moment to break his Victim silence. John shows his "I thirst" as uttered immediately before the triumphant "It is achieved." It would seem strange to have him at the climax of the redeeming sacrifice cease to speak as Priest in order to cry out his own anguish as Victim. There is anguish in the cry indeed. But surely it was the anguish of the race. In the Garden he had identified himself with the sinful

race of men. Now, as their Priest, offering himself for
their reconciliation with God, he spoke of the silence of
God which more than any other single thing stands an-
guishingly in the way of reconciliation.

5

The end of the three hours on the Cross is told
swiftly. Jesus said, "It is accomplished" (John 19.30) and
yielded up his spirit to the Father. We have heard him
say that there was to be a baptism in his own blood
(Luke 12.50), and it was a heavy strain waiting for it to
be accomplished (the same verb in Greek). Now it was
accomplished, the strain was over. He had come into the
world to *do* something, now he had done it.

Because a corpse must not be unburied at Passover,
his was placed in a tomb near Calvary, a tomb newly
cut, belonging to Joseph of Arimathea. Spices to be
strewn in the ledge and on the shroud were brought by
Nicodemus. He and Joseph were members of the Sanhedrin. They had kept their belief in Jesus secret, but now
in the hour of his failure proclaimed it—a thing as un-
likely in its way as the conversion of the thief.

Death did not hold Christ. It "was swallowed up in
victory," said Paul (1 Corinthians 15.54), quoting Isaiah.
On the third day—part of Friday, all of Saturday, part of
Sunday, three days by Jewish reckoning—the tomb was
found empty. It wasn't, as someone has wildly suggested, that they looked in the wrong tomb. Joseph of
Arimathea knew his own. It is characteristic of the
Evangelists that they do not tell us how Joseph reacted,
nor indeed is either Joseph or Nicodemus mentioned
again, important converts though they were. The New

Testament writers were not writing a chronicle, still less a Society Column, but the story of mankind's Redemption.

Of what happened on that first day and on the forty days (Acts 1.3) in which he came and went among them before his Ascension, the Evangelists selected, from their own memories and the accounts of others, incidents which they saw as specially significant, with no attempt to harmonize them. But all four give the same outline. There was the tomb found empty on the Sunday morning; there were appearances to various women, disciples, apostles.

When the news was first brought to the Eleven, they simply did not believe it, called it "an idle tale." Yet Jesus, when telling them of his suffering and death, had told of his rising again on the third day. Clearly they had assumed that whatever resurrection he was talking about would be in the next world, not bringing Jesus back, body and all, into this. His death would be—like the death of Abraham and Moses and David—the end of him here, themselves left mourning with only their memories, including the bleak memory of their own running away in Gethsemane.

The Christ who came back to them was the same Christ, but different too. His body was a real body, but the first time he came to them in the Upper Room, passing through a locked door, they thought he was a ghost: they "cowered down," full of the terror ghosts usually excite in healthy people. He urged them, "See my hands and my feet, that it is I myself; handle and see: for a spirit has not flesh and bones as you see me to have" (Luke 24.39). He ate a meal with them—"roast fish and honeycomb." Thomas was not there and flatly refused to believe those who were—"Until I have seen the marks of the nails in his hands, until I have put my finger into the mark of the nails, and put my hand into his side." A week later Jesus invited him to do precisely that (John 20.24–29)—and Thomas said, "My Lord and my God."

Yet there were times when they were not instantly sure it was he. Mary Magdalen had not at once recognized him that first Easter dawn in the Garden. The two disciples who walked with him to Emmaus did not know who their companion was till he "took bread and blessed and broke it, and offered it to them." On the mountain of the great commission to teach all nations, some were still doubtful (Matthew 28.17). Of the Emmaus pair Luke says, "Their eyes were held," Mark that "he appeared in the form of a stranger." It was his body, but glorified, free of the subjections matter imposes. He came and went, was seen and not seen, as he chose.

On his first appearance to the Eleven (John 20.22) he said, "Peace be to you." Is it pure chance that we have never heard him give them or anyone that greeting before, and now, with his reconciling work accomplished, we hear it three times? Then he breathed on them. This certainly was new: not only had he never done it before: in all the Old Testament no one had, since God breathed the breath of life into the nostrils of the man He had formed of dust from the ground. The breath Christ breathed was of a higher life and it prefaced the greatest change of all in him. For he said to them, "Receive the Holy Spirit"—the pneuma, the breath. Earlier we had read (John 7.39): "As yet the Spirit had not been given because Jesus was not yet glorified." Now we meet the risen Jesus, the Jesus who had learnt obedience by the things he suffered, and had been brought to "accomplishment," to the perfection of manhood that personal union with God the Son called for. His first gift to them was the Holy Spirit.

"He was now the source of salvation to all who obey him" (Hebrews 5.8). Salvation from what? From sin. And his second gift to the Apostles was the power to forgive sins and withhold forgiveness.

6

There was a time, and not so long ago, when the resurrection was used by the Christian apologist to prove Christ's divinity. It was a strange aberration. For Jesus himself warned us that there are those who would not believe, even if one rose from the dead (Luke 16.31).

In the opening speeches recorded in Acts, the Resurrection is thus emphasized. But then, it had happened in that very city only a couple of months before. As the years passed, the plain truth emerged that people will accept the Resurrection only if they already believe in the divinity—the divinity supports the Resurrection, not vice versa. Immediately after Christ's warning, the rulers proceeded to illustrate his statement by making the raising of Lazarus a reason for putting Jesus himself to death! And in our own days the principle still holds. Until men come to see Jesus as beyond the human measure, as at least in some degree divine, they will dismiss the story as an idle tale. There are pagan myths of resurrected gods, so they have read, and this is one more of them. Even those who do not refuse Christ some degree of acceptance use incredible ingenuity to escape accepting a genuine bodily resurrection, while not throwing the Gospels overboard. It is part of the general problem of those who can neither abandon the Gospels nor believe what they are saying. One reads, for instance, discussion of whether Jesus' Resurrection was "historical," setting up as a test a definition of history which very little of man's recording of the past would survive. How much of the story was fact, how much was later meditation, amounting to invention?

The New Testament leaves open no way of escape along those lines. After his death and burial, either Jesus did appear among his disciples, alive, in his body, or the whole thing is a lie. And only the occasional eccentric thinks that.

We have noted more than once that the Evangelists were not writing history; they were recording lived experience, things seen by themselves or men they knew. Read especially Corinthians 15. In 30 A.D. when Christ died and rose, Paul had been outside; he became a Christian five years after. We have already noted that in 57 he wrote to the Corinthians of a visit to them seven years earlier; he reminded them that he had told them that Christ died and was buried, "was raised on the third day, appeared to Cephas, then to the Twelve, then to more than five hundred brethren at one time, most of whom are still alive . . . then to James, then to all the apostles." Peter in his first speech on Pentecost day, there in Jerusalem seven weeks after the event (Acts 2.24), based the whole of his message on the Christ who had been killed and whom God had raised up—"of which we all are witnesses."

They know that they had seen, talked with, eaten with, the Christ who had died on the Cross. And they died for their certainty—James and Peter and Paul and so many others of them. None of the pagan myth-makers ever did that. But what did the Apostles think it all meant? How did they—guided, so Christ had promised, by the Holy Spirit—interpret their experience? We do not know how quickly, or with what aid from the Risen Christ, they realized that his death was sacrificial.

He had said that his dying was at his choice and for the sake of men. "I lay down my life for my sheep." Calvary was very near when he said, "The son of man . . . came to save others and give his life as a ransom for the lives of many" (Matthew 20.28)—"many" is a Hebraism, Jesus died for all men. At the Last Supper he said, "This is my blood of the new covenant which is shed for many for the forgiveness of sins" (Matthew 16.18)—all those at the Supper knew about "the blood of the covenant" which Moses had poured out (Exodus 24.6–8).

We never hear Jesus call his death a sacrifice, for that word we wait for Paul—"Christ our pasch is sacrificed" (1 Corinthians 5.7); "Christ has loved us and has delivered himself up for us, an oblation and a sacrifice to God" (Ephesians 5.2).

We tend to think of the Resurrection and the Ascension as simply happy sequels to Calvary. But more and more they have been seen as the sacrifice's necessary completion. All sacrifices for sin had meant the offering of a victim to God. Only a couple of times in the Old Testament did God show his acceptance of the sacrifice, by sending fire from heaven (Leviticus 9.24, 2 Chronicles 7.1). In this, the perfect sacrifice, of which all others were only prefigurings, God showed it by bringing the victim back to life. But with the Ascension God shows himself as accepting not only the sacrifice but the Victim. He took the Victim to himself: there was no way of doing that in the earlier sacrifices—what would God have done with a roasted ox or a blood-drained goat?

It was a perfect sacrifice, it was offered for the world's redemption. The trouble is that the world does not look redeemed!

Chapter XIV

Redemption Achieved

I

What were men redeemed from, what were they redeemed into?

Redemption is a strange word, for it means buying back: a man sold into slavery could be redeemed, a jewel pawned could be redeemed, the man liberated from his owner, the jewel from the pawnbroker. But Christ made his offering to God, and God knows what it cost him; and there could be no question of buying men back from God, liberating them from God. The whole point of Christ's sacrificial death was to bring men back *to* Him. Sin had made a division, and Christ healed it, making atonement, a word whose pronunciation masks its meaning. For it is at-one-ment, God and the human race now at one.

The word "redemption" was a key word of the Old Testament, where it meant the freeing of Israel from its sufferings here upon earth, since we cannot find in its Scriptures any awareness that man's destiny is to come into everlasting fullness of union with God. Paul, rabbinically trained, applied it to a redemption of which the Old Testament never dreamed. But the Gospel word is not redemption but salvation, not redeemer but saviour.

The other element that we owe to Paul is the relation of Christ's sacrifice to the sin of Adam. That also is not in the Gospels. That the breach between the human race and God went back to a sin at the race's origin is wholly probable, given what men are. The trouble is that if we bring in Adam, we shall be entangled in a discussion of evolution and never get back to redemption at all. That particular complication we escape in the book I am writing. Paul does indeed show Jesus splendidly and to me convincingly as the Second Adam. But the Second Adam never mentions the First.

The essential of what Christ did for men can be stated without reference to Genesis. It lies in two clear facts: (1) However man got that way, something is wrong with him: in the best of us there is a muddied mixture of vices and virtues: the thrust of self means that no one of us can be wholly relied on; (2) Jesus was different. Redemption means that we are lifted out of the kind of men we are into the possibility of being the kind of man Christ was. There it is in one sentence. To the end of our lives we shall never have worked out all that this sentence contains. But we can begin.

Jesus came to save his people from their sins. Sin is not in the ordinary sense of the word a failure to pay, it is a failure in doing, a failure in loving. "The man who commits sin violates order, sin is of its nature disorder" (1 John 3.4). It is not a question of a creditor to be paid, but of order to be restored. Sins are committed by individuals, but there really is a sin of the race, a solidarity in sin which is a parody of the solidarity in nature, the whole race involved in the wreck of things. In all there is failure in loving, refusal of love—love of self having its way against what we owe God, and what we owe others: even in what we owe ourselves. For we are at war within ourselves as evidently as against our neighbor. We can be torn any number of ways at once by desires which exclude one another. The passions harry man perpetually. That man should have passions is natural, he would be a poor thing without them: what is tragic is that they should dominate. Sex misused is not the most destructive of man's powers. It has been said of the United Nations Organization that it was a society of kettles on the boil. So potentially, and often enough in fact, is every human grouping—nation, family, casual groupings of every shape and size.

As we have noted, the Old Testament redemption was more this-worldly than Christ's but often draws close to his. Psalm 107 (106) gives a selection of "Those whom the Lord redeemed—hungry and thirsty, their souls fainted within them . . . some sat in darkness and gloom, prisoners in afflictions and in irons, for they had rebelled against the words of God . . . some were sick through their sinful ways, and because of their iniquities suffered affliction; they loathed any kind of food, they drew near to the gates of death." Then the superb climax, "They cried to the Lord in their trouble and he sent forth his word and healed them, and delivered them from destruction."

The chances are that most of those who have read the psalm, from its first writing to now, see all this as an excellent description of others, their own complacency unruffled. Jesus has a most frightening word about the complacent sinner, who goes about the business of living with no awareness of the disease of self that is eating him away: "As it was in the days of Lot—they ate, they drank, they bought, they sold, they planted, they built, but on the day when Lot went out from Sodom fire and brimstone rained from heaven and destroyed them all." And Sodom would have been spared if ten righteous men could have been found in it.

Christ's giving himself to death was the remedy for the disorder into which so endless a Niagara of sinning had brought mankind. It was not that Christ said to his Father: "All men deserve death. Would you mind killing me instead of them?" That would have been either horrifying or meaningless. What in effect he said was: "Because of my obedience in doing your will, teaching your will, attacking powerful men who are perverting your will, they are determined to kill me. Will you accept my death and apply it to the needs of all men?"

Christ's sacrifice was an answer to all the ways of man's refusal. Refusal of obedience was rectified in an act of limitless obedience, the final effort Christ himself had to make was in the "not my will but thine" of Gethsemane. Refusal of man to give himself to God was balanced on Calvary by a limitless self-giving. And all this happened in a human soul and body, Jesus draining his human resources in an act as human as the sins it was offered to redeem, his divinity not called on to save him a single throb of suffering. In the man Christ Jesus the offering annihilated all that lay between man and God.

In the man Christ Jesus. But how did the effect of it reach the rest of men? For it did. At the Last Supper, Christ had stated what Redemption was to mean—"I in my Father and you in me and I in you." That is what man is redeemed into—the union of men with God in Christ.

2

Christ himself says that he lays down his life for his flock (John 10.15–18) and that he does it out of love for his Father and his fellow men: "Therefore does the Father love me, because I lay down my life that I may take it up again. No one takes it from me." But what connection is there between his suffering and our healing?

We might very well have received the benefit simply because Christ asked the Father that we should, and we should have no complaint had that been the way of it. But it was not. He was not, so to speak, handing his Father an infinite check and saying, "Pay their debt out of that." It would have been generous, but with a generosity laced with contempt, a touch of kindness to animals almost: as if he were saying "Poor devils, we can't expect much of them." In fact men were to be changed, not only redeemed but given the possibility of sanctification (1 Corinthians 1.30), "delivered from the dominion of darkness and transferred to the kingdom of his beloved Son."

Yet men are not to be passive recipients of another's anguish. The breach between our race and God no one but Christ could have healed. But with that accomplished, each must still work out his own personal redemption "in fear and trembling"—as indeed Jesus had worked out the redemption of their race. Redemption is not a labor-saving device. It does not make men's salvation easy, it only makes it possible. Nor is Christ handing down gifts to men's lowliness from his height, but bringing them into real oneness with himself. As Paul wrote to the Ephesians, God "Chose us in Jesus Christ before the foundation of the world . . . destined us in love to be his sons through Jesus Christ. . . . *In* him we have redemption through his blood, the forgiveness of our sins" (1.3). "Before the foundation of the world." There is a new time dimension. Redemption is for all men from the beginning.

One hears the objection raised: "The human race is half a million years old. The notion that at the Last Judgment every man that has ever lived will rise again, body and all, is sheer fantasy. It's science fiction, not religion."

Religion, of course, *is* stranger than science fiction, which can but limp after the realities religion glimpses. What underlies the objection is a profound conviction that individual men don't matter. But from the men of the dawn half a million years ago (if that's the date!) to the child born today, every man matters. They are all made by God in His own image, every one of them has an immortal soul, and there is not one of them for whom Christ did not die.

There may have been animal forms on the way to man, quarter men, half men, almost-men, but once men have arrived, something new is in the world, with a function in God's plan for the world. No single one of them was a mere transient, a stage on the way to something else, to be cast into the discard. We may feel some of our earlier ancestors primitive: but to the gaze of the infinite God even our Shakespeares and Einsteins, to say nothing of you and me, are not so very advanced. The earliest men may be far distant from us, but they and we are equi-distant from God—which means equi-present to God.

3

As we have seen, we are to be changed from the kind of men we are into the kind of man Jesus became in his death and resurrection. We are born as members of the human race, we are reborn as members of Christ. There is profound mystery here. It goes back to that deep point of his agony in Gethsemane when he identified himself with sinful mankind. There is nothing else in human experience for light-giving comparison. We can only stammer, as Paul did when he said: "He became sin for us." He took the weight of man's sinfulness on himself, and it all but killed him before ever the Temple guard could reach him.

The weight of sin? Not the guilt at least, that goes with the actual sinning and cannot be transferred. Read Isaiah 53 again, the chapter to which he referred the Apostles at the Last Supper. He took on himself the realization of the foulness of what we his brothers have done from the beginning, the sorrow for sin that we should have felt but did not feel. He could not have known what he was taking upon himself till it came upon him. On the Cross, as I once wrote, "He bore the burden of the sin he was expiating in a profound identification with man at the point where man most needed redemption"—surely the desolation of the sinful humanity with whom he had chosen to be identified was what his cry of forsakenness by God was uttering.

In that sense all men from the beginning of time till the end are associated with his Passion and Death. So Paul could say, "With Christ I am nailed to the Cross"

(Galatians 2.20). And therefore the fruits of Passion and Death are theirs by right, unless they refuse them. So Paul could say, "It is no longer I who live, but Christ lives in me." Life is the key, newness of life.

One might read the whole story of redemption in two texts—the first we have already dwelt on: "I in my Father and you in me and I in you." The second we must consider as closely, "Unless a man is born again he cannot see the kingdom of God."

We cannot long study the first Christians without realizing that they were living a double life and contemplating a double death. There was the life all men have, and the death all men must die. But Paul refers more often to another life—not a life to be entered on at our death but lived here parallel with the first. It has its own death, of which the man may be unaware in the sheer liveliness of the first life: "The wages of sin is death," but the sinner who has received that wage may feel very lively indeed. Theologians have come to speak of natural life, the life we have simply by being men, life in Adam, so to speak, and supernatural life, life in Christ. *Charis* Paul calls it (a free gift, grace in English); so does Peter, who tells husband and wife that they are "heirs together of the grace of life."

For a second life we might expect a second birth. And that is what John records Jesus as telling Nicodemus we must have. "Unless a man is born again he shall not see the kingdom of God" (John 3.3): birth is entry into life, re-birth is entry into another life. John, we remember, wrote his Gospel in order that "we might know that Jesus is the Christ, the Son of God, and that believing we might have life in his name." The truth that this other life was the whole point of Jesus' coming was especially living in John. As part of his own meditation on life with Jesus—and on life as son to Jesus' mother—he had spoken in his first chapter of a birth men are to have, not in the order of nature, by blood or flesh or man's will, but by the will of God. In that birth those who have accepted the Word-made-flesh become children of God.

In John's third chapter the Word-made-flesh himself says to Nicodemus the words we have quoted about a second birth. The idea was so wholly new to Nicodemus —it is nowhere in the Old Testament—that he thought Jesus meant getting back into the womb, a feat in which he saw practical difficulties. Jesus told him that the second birth was by water and the Holy Spirit—baptism, in fact.

There are two ideas John quotes Jesus as uttering: a generation before John wrote, Paul takes both ideas for granted, so that even the sceptical are coming to suspect that Jesus did in fact utter them. One is this idea of a new life—"I am come that they may have life and have it more abundantly" was not a reference to health or longevity. The second is the idea of indwelling, inliving. The life is not something he gives us, as our parents gave us theirs, "I *am* the life," he said at the Last Supper. If he had said "I have the life," we could have asked him, "Please give it to us." But he is the life. We can only ask him to live in us.

The phrase we have already quoted is one example —"You in me and I in you"—but that is not the only time he speaks of the necessity of his living in us and our living in him. In the order of nature it is only in a living body that this two-way inliving is found—I can say the cells of my body live in me, I can say I live in the cells of my body, since it is only with my life that they live. So we find Paul comparing the Christian Church to a body: what makes a body is the one life principle by which every element in it lives. In the Church the one life that all share is Christ's. "Baptized in Christ, we have *put on Christ,*" Paul says to the Galatians (3.27). Paul struggles to find ways of making clear the extraordinary thing he is saying. "If anyone is in Christ, he is a new creation" (2 Corinthians 5.17). "Put on the new nature created after the likeness of God" (Ephesians 4.21). In the Second Epistle of Peter the ultimate word in this order is said—"We are to be made partakers of the divine nature" (1.14)—the Second Person of the Trinity shares our humanity, we are to share His divinity.

Paul of course could not have imposed so new a concept on the Church of which he was so new a member. It could only have come from Jesus himself. And John tells us that it did. Where Paul uses a body and its limbs, Jesus uses a vine and its branches. Read John 15.1–12. "I am the vine, you are the branches. He who abides in me, and I in him, bears much fruit." A condition of our living in him, effectively, fruitfully, is that his words abide in us; a second condition is that we keep his commandments.

"Living with Christ's life" does not involve parrot-like imitation. We remain ourselves, with our own natural gifts and temperaments. Because he scourged money-changers out of the Temple, we need not feel called upon for similar violences, though some of us may. Paul asks us to be imitators of him as he is of Christ. But every man, including Paul, will have his own way of being like Christ—more or less, alas, none of us perfectly, some of us unrecognizably, to any eye but his.

It is the second life, the super-natural life, that we share with him. He was indwelt by the Holy Spirit, so must we be. The Holy Spirit is to be living and operative in us as in him—the only limit being our own willingness to receive him.

Because the humanity of the Christ whom we have "put on," into whom we have been incorporated (the metaphors vary), is united with God the Son and so with Father and Holy Spirit, so is ours. From the beginning of our universe the Persons of the Trinity are present in all things whatsoever, maintaining them in existence. But in members of Christ's body they "indwell," make their home. A body indwelt by a spiritual soul is a new reality beyond the animal, so a man indwelt by God is in Paul's words a new creation. The second life of the re-born man, the life of grace, is the "natural" life of man thus super-naturalized. Faith, hope and charity are the normal powers of the "indwelt" man.

For every kind of life there is food of its own kind. Bodily life is nourished by matter, by meat or vegetables, not by ideas. The spirit's life must be nourished by spiritual food, ideas, not meat or vegetables. For the life which is Christ, the food is Christ. In the Blessed Eucharist we receive Christ himself. There has been much argument recently about the Real Presence, with meanings suggested for Presence which would mean that we are not receiving Christ himself. But the phrase Real Presence is not in the Gospels. What Christ said was "This is my body." Needless to say there are new meanings suggested for "body," making it mean just about anything but body. But it would be hard to apply them to "This is the cup of my blood." One is puzzled at the reluctance to give their plain meaning to words uttered so close to death. That there should be a way of uniting

Christ to ourselves bodily might seem too good to be true: but surely only a Manichee would thrust away the possibility as repellent.

4

Christ has made it clear that the fullness of manhood will not be in this life. Death comes between. Death, which took him but could not hold him, will take us but will not hold us. As he rose we shall rise. *Because* he rose we shall rise. "I go to prepare a place for you." Read again the fifteenth chapter of First Corinthians. We shall rise body and soul.

This is a glorification of the human body which the materialist cannot abide: according to the degree of his seriousness it stirs him to anger or amusement. "If an explorer is eaten by a cannibal, how can both their bodies rise again at the end of the world?" There we have a specimen of a hundred jokes levelled at the truth that at the world's end we shall be reconstituted as complete men, body and soul. Warming to his theme, the objector-humorist may have a number of cannibals eating different slices of the explorer, and being eaten in their turn, some by tigers, some by crocodiles, some by sharks, some by other cannibals.

All this is good fun, but it is based on a misunderstanding of what is meant by "the same body." Scientists tell us that every few years all the cells of our body have gone their way and been replaced by others like themselves. So it is not only cannibals that eat men's bodies, time eats them too; and whereas the cannibal eats a given human body once for all, time does it again and again. No single piece of matter that went to make up my body ten years ago is there now.

Yet it is the same body—same likes and dislikes, same skills, same incompetences, same memories above all, pleasures diminishing, pains multiplying, memory dimming, but my body all the way through. The continuing life-principle in me carries with it some power enabling it to confer an identity on the ever-changing matter of my body. It is this same power, but at a new level of intensity, that will be in operation at the Resurrection.

What is strange is that the "how" of our resurrection should loom so much larger in our interest than the fact of it. Even those who are not given to Scripture reading have heard the words "The resurrection of the body" all their lives in the Apostles' Creed. And Scripture is full of it. How it will function, this risen body, we do not know. Shall we find ourselves saying, "That must be Jones, I'd know his nose anywhere"? To speculate like this may be entertaining, and there is no harm in it provided we recognize that it's only speculation. The scholars indeed are having a grammarians' carnival over the Scriptural meaning of "soma," "psyche," "pneuma"—body, soul, spirit. I call it a carnival because they are so evidently enjoying themselves, but one feels they are making real progress.

Yet if anyone lets himself be worried by the question what body we shall be wearing at the Resurrection, St. Paul has a word for him in the same fifteenth chapter (verse 36). "Poor fool," he calls him. He continues with the analogy of seed sown in the ground and the very different harvest which grows from it. "What you sow is not the full body that is one day to be, it is only bare grain . . . it is for God to embody it according to his will."

So the separation of soul and body at death is not

final. And it is not final because God really *meant* man. That union of matter and spirit—which we call spirit embodied, or body enspirited—has a permanent place in God's plan. Without man, there would be a world of spirit and a world of matter, two worlds. Man, belonging to both, locks them into one world. And what God has thus joined together, He will not finally put asunder. For ever it will be humanity's function to hold the two in oneness.

What life will be like in the risen body we cannot know in detail. It has not been shown to us, indeed much of it could not be shown to us—any more than the activities of man's mature mind and full grown body can be explained to a child. How strange we find what we are told about the one risen body that has been seen in our world, Christ's own. Yet certain primary things we know.

Man's *integrity* will have been restored, and at a new level of realized contact with God. "What is sown corruptible, rises incorruptible; what is sown unhonored, rises in glory; what is sown in weakness is raised in power." The warfare within us will be over—the body so wholly responsive to spirit that St. Paul can call it a "spiritual body," and the spirit wholly responsive to God. Every energy in us will be functioning at its fullest upon its supreme object, and wholly nourished in its functioning. There is no better definition of delight.

When will the body rise again? The answer of the New Testament as a whole is that it will happen at the end of the world, when Christ returns to make that full accounting of the whole human race which is called the Last Judgment. The parousia, and the reign of anti-

Christ before it, I do not discuss because they do not make that difference to us here and now which is our concern in this book. That there will be a life for men between death and the resurrection of the body seems quite clear. The body goes to disintegration and corruption at death, but life continues. That in man which knows and loves will grow to fullness in the direct knowledge and love of Father, Son and Holy Spirit. There is much theorizing about an element which links soul and body, which makes our body the same body through all the changes it goes through on earth. If there is such an element, does it survive with the soul?

Death Christ shows as a decisive moment. "If hand or foot or eye cause one to sin, then cut off hand or foot, pluck out eye"—so far he is using a proverb already existent. But the deadly serious part is not in the proverb —"It is better for you to enter life maimed or lame than with two hands or feet be cast into the eternal fire. . . . It is better for you to enter life with one eye than with two eyes to be cast into the hell of fire."

"The body goes into the ground in weakness, it is raised in power," says St. Paul. What will the new power be? We cannot know because, while we know the seed (these bodies of ours) only too well, we have not seen the fruit; and we remember how St. Paul dismisses as half-witted the effort to argue from what the seed is to what the fruit will be like. The one thing certain is that the fullness of human life, social as well as individual, lies beyond the gateway of death. Yet all that we have learned here from our strengths and weaknesses, our successes and failures, will be producing its own rich fruit in that new life. It is not only our bodies that will rise again, but our whole life. We shall at last be fully men and not, as here, the raw material out of which men are being made.

But we must co-operate in our own making, and not spend so much energy in unmaking ourselves. What of those whose whole energy has resulted in their unmaking, God and their neighbor alike excluded from their love, so that they have excluded themselves from the kingdom? What will their continuing misery mean to those who are in bliss? We have not been told. There is only speculation, and some of it very unpleasing, making God a monster. To one thing we can hold: God is Love. If we arrive at any answer to the problem of everlasting refusal which is irreconcilable with Love, or has nothing in common with anything that men can recognize as Love, what have we gained? Only a form of words.

Christ has talked of heaven as entering into life, life in the joy of his Father. But he has given no more detail of the joy than of the fire which is its bleak alternative. We are not to think of those in heaven as basking in an endlessness of blissful stagnation—the kind of thing that Karl Marx's friend Engels dismissed so scornfully as "the tedium of personal immortality." That would not be life. Men will be alive as they have never been. And they will be men still, not only soul and body united, but with the social fact of human nature—that human beings need one another and would be incomplete without one another—functioning at the new level of glorified soul and glorified body. They will have such energies in them as they have never known, and these energies will be fruitful.

One has heard descriptions of heaven—harps and

hymns and holy shouting—which make it seem like a rather spectacular church service. As a result, we Christians are thought to be saying that provided we give up all the sins which might make life a little more bearable, at the end, as a reward, we shall be admitted into a church service and never allowed out. As people have been given to understand that hell is even worse, many of them decide not to think about what follows death, but concentrate on making the best of things here; which means that they are living towards nothing in particular, and what could be more devitalizing than that?

But the notion of heaven which has attracted them so little uses only the imagery of Scripture, and leaves out the reality. The life of heaven is expressed in the New Testament as *seeing*. Our Lord talks of the angels who see the face of his heavenly Father continually. St. John says that "we shall see him as he is." St. Paul says that "we shall see no longer in a mirror but face to face." Every last one of us is made in God's image: in heaven the image will be looking the original full in the face! We shall not simply know *about* God, we shall know God. We shall not simply have an idea of God as we do here, only fuller and richer: God himself, seen to be God, will have taken the place of the idea of God in our minds. Our knowing power will have reached its own perfection and beyond, our loving power will have moved up to the same new level.

This heaven of ours may at first hearing sound a little thin and remote, too exclusively spiritual; we may feel that it is all very noble, but a poor substitute for the more robust joys we have known on earth. We may even imagine ourselves in heaven looking back wistfully to the dear dead joys of beef and beer. But we should be fooling ourselves. It is as though a small boy marvelled that grown-ups should spend their time with poetry or science or girls, ignoring the tin soldiers and cowboy outfit and rockinghorse of his own present ecstasy. To feel like that about heaven is to assume that we shall stay eternally retarded at our present level of development.

We shall not be absorbed in the Infinite, merged in it, our own self forever lost in it like a drop in an ocean. We shall be wholly ourselves as we have never been: we shall know in ourselves at last the perfect harmony of soul and body, for the body too will rise again. And we shall be joined in a community of knowledge and love with our fellow men, such as we have never dreamed of here.

For, just as the goal for each individual is to grow to full perfection as a man, so the goal for the human race is to grow to full perfection as a community, mirroring the perfect community of Father, Son and Holy Spirit in whose image we all are created. In organic union with Christ, this community will include not only—as all the Utopias do—all who happen to be living at a particular moment, but all men that ever have lived and have refused to make self their God.

Chapter XV

"Always Living to Make Intercession"

I
Towards the end of the three hours on the Cross comes an incident, strangely worded: "Jesus, knowing that all was now *finished,* said (to *fulfil* the scripture) 'I thirst.' . . . They put a sponge full of vinegar on hyssop to his mouth. When Jesus had received the vinegar, he said 'It is *finished';* and he bowed his head and gave up his spirit." (John 19.28–30) This is the Revised Standard Version.

It must have been a difficult passage to translate, because the three italicized words, "finished" (twice) and "fulfil," all come from the same Greek verb. We have already met it—"There is a baptism with which I must be baptized, and how am I constrained till it be *accomplished."* We are to meet it again in Hebrews, twice. The first: "He learned obedience through what he suffered; and being *made perfect"* . . . (5.8–9). The second tells that the prophets and heroes of the Old Testament "did not receive what was promised, since God had foreseen something better for us, that apart from us they should not be *made perfect"* (11.40).

215

One feels that the basic meaning is of something "accomplished" on Calvary, which the word "finished" does not very well convey—something accomplished in Christ, something to find accomplishment in us.

Certainly his redemptive activity was not finished, in the sense of being over. "He entered heaven *on our behalf,*" says Hebrews. There was something he still had to do for men, and Paul told the Romans what it was— "Christ Jesus . . . at the right hand of God intercedes for us." Hebrews sets this out in more detail: "He holds his priesthood permanently, so he is able for all time to save those who draw near to God *through him,* since he always lives to make intercession" (7.24). On Calvary, as mediator, he reconciled the human race with the Father, healed the division sin had made. That was done once and for all. It needed no redoing. In heaven, once slain upon Calvary, now forever living, he presents himself to his Father as an "intercession." So Romans and Hebrews both show. He is interceding, praying, for what? That what has been won for all should be made available to each, accepted by each, not refused by any. For Christ's death no more makes men holy than the sin at the beginning of the race, whatever it was, made men sinful. Both altered the conditions in which men had to live their lives, make their decisions, choose their direction. Christ made salvation possible, but each for himself must join with Christ in making it actual. There is no one, from the beginning of time till the end, who cannot be saved, no one who cannot refuse: acceptance or refusal is ours: it is the whole point of our lives, in each detail and in their totality.

Redemption as sacrifice then, was completed on Cal-

vary: Redemption as the application of Calvary's sacrifice is continuous. As completed, Redemption was the
work of Christ alone. As continuous, it is the work of
Christ, but he uses men too. We noted at the beginning
of this book that what we have just seen as Christ's
continuing intercession breaks through to our altars in
the Mass: the priest, by the command, and in the power,
of Christ, offers the same Christ sacramentally present,
to the same Father for the same purpose—that all men
may be given the light and the strength to find salvation
in Calvary. For, Catholics see, the Mass is Calvary as
Christ now offers it to his Father. We join with the
priest, and so with Christ, in making the offering. It is
the most important thing we ever do. And how difficult
we find it to realize that!

2

This matter of the Mass is a special example of the
other side of the truth about the Mystical Body of Christ.
So far we have been considering it as the way in which
the cells of the Body live with the life of Christ whose
Body the Church is. But a body exists not for the sake of
its cells, but for the completeness and service of the
person. The Mystical Body is not there that we may have
a healthy, well-nourished spiritual life. It is there because there is a work still to be done in the world which
Christ does through it, for which in the strictest sense he
needs it.

Consider his comparison of himself to a Vine. The
branches of a vine are not like the branches of a business. A vine does not decide to found some branches and
keep a protective eye on them, thus providing employ-

ment for some who would otherwise lack it. The branches are in the first place an extension of the vine's life, in the second they are necessary for the vine's productiveness—no branches, no grapes! Notice what Paul says (1 Corinthians 12.21) of the companion metaphor of the Body: "The head cannot say to the feet, I have no need of you." Remember who the head is!

For Redemption on Calvary, Christ needed only himself. But for the continuation of his work among men till the end of time he needs the Church. Christ in the Body is the whole Christ. Through the Body he carries on the work of bringing men to his Father. In his power the members of the body, the cells, teach and give the sacraments, pray and offer Mass, suffer and offer their sufferings to be united with his and used for the help and healing of others. In that sense the Church—call it the Mystical Body, call it the Kingdom, call it the People of God—is Christ continuing to work in the world through a social body as he once worked in the world through the body in which he was conceived and born and lived in Palestine, died and rose from death and lives with his Father in heaven.

The question of the nature of the Church Christ founded divides Christians. But certain principles, I think, are common to all. The union of men with God in Christ we have seen as Redemption achieved. I can hardly imagine a Church which would not consider that as the formula for its own self. If Christ is not living in a Church, continuing his redeeming activity in it, uniting men to God in it, helping other men towards the same union, what do its members see as the point of it?

The work of teaching and offering we have touched upon several times. Let us glance at the "work" of suffering. That we shall suffer is one of life's certainties. What Christ has shown is that suffering need not be wasted. There is indeed pointless suffering in our world, but suffering need not be pointless.

From the standpoint of the casual onlooker, which is that of more and more of his followers today, nothing could have been more pointless than his own death—an enraged God demanded blood and Jesus gave it. But that was not how it was. There is an organic connection between suffering and the healing of sin. Sin is the thrust of our own will away from right and good. The reversal of that thrust, turning the will back from the evil it craves, can only cause us suffering. In that sense suffering is not the demand of an angry judge, but the prescription of a physician bent upon our healing. And that surely was what Jesus meant by saying that all of us must take up our cross daily.

But suffering is not only necessary for our own healing. In the Body the suffering of one may be applied to the healing of another. There is a co-redemptive suffering in which we are all called upon to share. Listen to Paul: "I rejoice in my sufferings for your sake, and in my flesh I complete what is lacking in Christ's afflictions for the sake of his body, that is the Church" (Colossians 1.24). The sentence is doubly stunning, for Paul not only speaks of something lacking in Christ's sufferings but says that he, Paul (and presumably other Christians), will "complete" them for the sake of Christ's body, the Church. Whatever the God-man could do, Christ did. What was lacking could only be something which in the nature of the case could not be done by the God-man for men but must be done by men for themselves. Men are not merely to be spectators of their own redemption.

Purely human love, yours and mine, is not to be denied all place in the expiation of human sin.

That in the Mystical Body we are in the full tide of Christ's life is a thought wholly joyous. But that the Body exists to do the work Christ wants done is very sobering. A weakness in any cell obstructs the Body's effectiveness. Evil in high places—in Popes and Curia and Hierarchy—can not only hinder the work for which Christ assumed a body, but can dim and distort Christ's face as the world sees it. Catholics can become speechless with fury as they think of things their leaders have done or failed to do, through the ages and now. But I have already spoken of the man I know who cannot get his share of pleasure out of the tongue-lashing of our leaders, because he cannot think of their ways of failing Christ without beginning to think of his own. After all, the world at large tends to judge the Church not by Popes or World Councils but by the Christians it actually sees. If only there were no Christians (we find ourselves feeling), the whole world would be converted!

But Christ knew that one of his first group would betray him, that another would deny him, that through the ages scandals would come—that the chair of Peter, for instance, would be occupied by successors of the Peter who drew the sword, the Peter who ran away, the Peter who denied, as well as of the Peter who confessed his sinfulness to Jesus by the Lake and accepted Paul's rebuke at Antioch, the Peter who preached the first sermons on and after Pentecost day, the Peter who baptized Cornelius, the Peter who was martyred.

Yet he entrusted his work in the world to men.

Chapter XVI

The Practicality of Jesus

We are to have the mind of Christ, Paul tells us—not simply his great deeds and his great words and his loving kindness but the mind from which deeds and words and loving kindness issued. We must see as he saw, must live mentally in the reality in which he lived. His mental world was God-filled. So must ours be. As a beginning let us ponder a while on why it matters to the world now trying to be born that God should be not only accepted and honored but constantly present to us, so that to see anything at all without in the same act seeing God means to see it as it is not.

I

I remember a pleasing *New Yorker* cartoon—a father looks up from his small son's school report and says to the shivering child, "Now you go right back in there and integrate." "Integration" had not at that time become the decisive word in Black-White relations. It applied to social relations generally. In this sense it is still one of the key clichés of our world, used as often as "relevance" and "meaningfulness," and as rootless as these. For where is the integrated society, whether of

221

small boys or grown men, in whose completeness and clarity we are to rediscover our own?

To Christ, as to psalmist and prophet, it was no cliché, because it was rooted in God, who is the only integer, wholly himself, the whole of himself. But men today can say integration without giving a thought to "integer," just as they can say Christmas without giving a thought to Christ or Mass. Even devoted Christians today seem instinctively to avoid those two towering radicals, God and Christ. We are told that the object of Penance is to reconcile us, that is re-integrate us, not with God, not with Christ, but with the Christian community. And how integrated with either God or Christ is the Christian community? Our own parish, for instance—on the average is it any more integrated with God than we are ourselves? And what does it mean to us to be reintegrated with its semi-integration? For it and for us God is the integer, and Christ is the way to integration with him.

If the believer is thus in danger of seeing reality shapeless because God is left out of account, what shape can reality have to a non-believer, whether he be a man totally without belief or a once-believer for whom the fading of the old certainties has left life meaningless and himself emptied of hope? Without God—and God seen as concerned and in action—the universe is literally meaningless, for there is no mind to mean it. It is simply there, an accident which happened to happen with men simply parts of the happening which have emerged late. There is no totality in it, no wholeness, merely countless myriads of individual bits and pieces, no "all," only the sum of the things that happen to be. There is no purpose in it, simply a drift of things expanding (as most scientists seem to think) towards a state of maximum entropy, which means an inertness equivalent to death since nothing whatever can happen in it: unless of course it begins to contract again to a point at which it might start all over again on a career as meaningless.

This does not mean that life to a non-believer must be purposeless. Men are not made like that. Anyone can think up for himself a purpose in a universe thus going nowhere in particular—a purpose selfish or selfless or that uneasy mixture of both which we all know so well. He can perhaps get others to work with him towards its achievement. But he will vanish from the scene, and so will these others: and what will their successors make of what they may have managed to achieve? What would Lenin have thought of Stalin? The one thing reasonably to be counted on is the thrust of the self, each individual thrusting towards his own satisfactions, and what becomes of integration?

With no agreed principles, the world trying to be born cannot get itself born, it can only go on altering disintegration's present shape. For, once again, what can integration mean when there is no integer? And if there is no mind as the source of the whole movement of the universe and no mind as its goal, what integer can there be? The new generation of men are born, each individual with his own self as a disintegrating principle to be controlled or merely indulged. There will be rare minds with their own vision of what ought to be done and how, with ever and again the sense of futility draining energy as if they were at best decorating their cabin in a sinking ship. There will be the mass of mindless men taking life as it comes, grasping satisfaction as it offers, on the model of "Captain Brown, who played his ukulele as the ship went down." And over all, the leering face of the Psalmist's fool saying, and not only in his heart, "There is no God."

For the psalmists felt that God was the whole point, and so did the prophets. So John saw, and Paul. In Jesus, what prophets and psalmists were feeling towards lived among us. From Jesus, John and Paul got the vision of reality which they wrote down for us. It does involve integration of men with one another, but rooted in, drawing life from, integration with God. Without him integration is baby talk. And our way to him is Jesus of Nazareth—a key fact which too many earnest Christians have forgotten, because all today's talk is of the commandment he called the Second.

I am reminded of a noisy heckler at a religious meeting on a London street-corner. To a speaker he had already maddened by continuous interruption, he said: "Your church has been in existence for two thousand years, and look at the state of the world." The speaker said: "Water has been in existence since the beginning of time and look at the state of your neck!" He should not have said it, of course: one should never raise a laugh at the expense of a questioner: the more annoying he is, the more he needs the Faith. But the answer had two elements of justice in it.

The first is that to be effective water must be actually applied to the body and religion to the soul: it is no argument against the cleansing power of either that they cleanse only those who use them. The second is that the cleansing of body and soul alike begins with each man at birth—no neck has been subjected to water for millions of years, no soul to the Church for two thousand years. Each is a new problem—the soul especially, with the will in it which can choose what itself wants and not what God wants. My struggle with temptation has to be my own, not obviously helped by the successful struggle of sinners before I was born.

But there is more to the question. The Second Vatican Council reminds us that Redemption was to mean a renewal of the temporal order too. If the world really was redeemed by Our Lord so long ago, ought it not to show some sign of it? Ought it not to be a better world now than then? And isn't it in fact a worse one?

Whether the world ought, in the questioner's sense, to be better depends on what Redemption was meant to accomplish: we shall come back to that. But let us glance at whether it is in fact better or worse. The answer might seem to call for a degree of learning that no man has, weighing up life as it was lived then at every level in every country, comparing it with life as it is lived now. There are vaster horrors now—six million Jews exterminated in gas chambers, for instance; a hundred thousand Japanese slain by two atom bombs; the present threat of the destruction of the whole human race. But these mean only that scientific progress has put vaster powers of destruction in men's hands, not that men are worse. Nero or Heliogabalus or Tamurlane would not have shrunk from mass destruction on any scale whatever.

For the rest, the balance at least in the Western world, the one I know, seems to be in favor of *now* as against *then*. Every evil that effects our world—millions of our own people below the subsistence level for instance, national prejudice, color prejudice, religious prejudice, strong exploiting weak—can be matched in the world before Christ. And there is much good that is new. Inhumanity exists still, but it no longer exists unquestioned: masses of men are horrified at it and in revolt against it. Governments that still use torture as a political weapon try to hide it from world opinion.

Describing slavery in the Roman Empire (which was by no means the worst the world has known) the great historian Mommsen said that all the sufferings of all the slaves in the Southern United States were only a drop in the bucket by comparison. In most of our world, slavery (the ownership of men by other men) not only no longer exists, it is quite unthinkable: wage slavery has its own horrors, but lesser and more curable. And in a score of other fields—the position of women, the position of children, judicial torture, education, famine relief, hospitals and medical care (to name only a handful)—there is improvement. Compared with the ideal, the gains may seem pitifully small. But compared with what in the past men have actually had, the gains are solid. But not solid enough to support the notion, uttered by Bonhoeffer and widely repeated, that mankind has come of age. The technologists, who have such mastery in the handling of the material universe and hope soon to be able to remake man according to any recipe that pleases them, are for the most part "lost"— in the sense of Chapter V. They do not know why anything is here or what comes next. Lostness is no part of maturity's definition. Vatican II is nearer reality when it says mankind has reached a crisis point in its progress towards maturity.

In such advances as there have been Christ has

played a vast part. But is it by this that his success or failure is to be measured? Our answer must be that vital as it is, it is secondary. For it concerns man's relation to man. Redemption's primary concern was—is—with man's relation to God. The answer may well sound flat and evasive—men's relations with one another seem so very close and real, their relation to God seems remote and unreal in comparison.

But if the God-relation is not right, the man-relation cannot be. Jesus himself said, *"Seek first* the kingdom of God, and all these things will be added to you." Today there is a real, a heart-warming, striving for "all these things." But there is small sign of what Christ stated as the condition for success. Any legislator who so much as mentioned the kingdom of God would be laughed out of public life. Yet without God it is not possible to know what life is all about, men cannot know how they should handle their own lives or anyone else's.

2

Without knowing where either the individual or the race is supposed to be going, how is either to get there? I for one would not know how to live life intelligently: I could only play it by ear, and only so long as I had an ear. From Christ we know the purpose of life and where the road leads that men are on, we know what success is and what failure is and what each of these means to ourselves. Not that knowing settles everything. We still have the whole battle of life to fight, but at least our feet are on firm ground. The practical problems of living are no easier to solve. Self-interest tugs at us just as hard. Our particular sins do not lose their attractiveness. But in the fighting of any battle it is helpful to know what victory actually is: to say nothing of what we ourselves are.

Upon this last there is no agreed answer in our world. There are those who think man is a union of matter and spirit; those who think he is matter only, but developing; those who think he is spirit, with his body no more than a temporary disfigurement from which one day he will be free (*soma sema,* said the Greeks, the body is a tomb); there are those who think he is no more than a replaceable spare part in the collective machine.

Among those four positions you have utter disagreement. And most people have not as much "position" as the least of these: enough for them that they know a man when they see one—two legs, no feathers, I suppose: which means that they know what a man looks like but not what he is, which means that he does not know what he is himself, a most miserable kind of poverty.

Yet, apart from the satisfaction of a quite reasonable curiosity about ourselves, does the knowledge make any practical difference? It makes a dozen differences, all very practical indeed. Consider three of them. Unless we know what a man is—not this man or that, but any man simply *as* a man—we do not know what a man's value is, what his rights are, and whether there is any meaning at all in human equality. These things are being called in question all the time, and the whole future of our race depends on giving them the right answers.

Being nice people we can *say* that every man is of value simply for being a man, but unless we can say what a man is, we have no answer at all to those who regard men as no more than replaceable spare parts in the social machine. Upon the question of human rights, we are on no better ground: for rights are not whatever we should like to have, whatever we can manage to seize for ourselves, or whatever those in power are willing to concede us. Rights are what we are entitled to *as men*—but what *are* men? And what does human equality mean? Men are not equal in any quality that we can name—intelligence, energy, courage, kindness: the one thing all men have in common is that they are men: but what is a man? We cannot build much on the number of legs and the featherlessness. Unless being a man is of such value *in itself* that it outweighs all the natural qualities in which men differ, the equality of men is only a slogan.

The Christian knows what a man is. Consider one saying of Christ's: "Fear not those who can kill the body, but cannot kill the soul." This means that man is a union of matter and spirit: meant for (but able to refuse) everlasting life in union with God. Add to the definition that Christ died for him. And we can add two further enrichments—man is what God the Son could become, what the Holy Spirit can indwell. And these truths apply to all men from the beginning.

For one enormous practical value of this knowledge, let us apply it to the problem of human equality. No one who knew what he was saying could possibly say, "That man is immortal, as I am, but I am better born than he": the words would perish in the utterance from their sheer idiocy—the superiority in birth that he claims being so tiny a thing compared with the immortality in which he admits equality. For the same reason one could not say: "Christ died for that man, as he died for me, but my skin is a better color than his."

The Christian view of what man is makes every man an object of respect. Indeed it goes deeper than that: it makes him an object of reverence. And it is our sad experience that what we do not reverence we shall profane. If we do not reverence man, we shall profane men —profane other men, profane ourselves.

Indeed Christians, who know these truths about man, have betrayed them often enough, betrayed them callously, horribly. But the truths are there, and carry their own corrective.

Knowing our purpose in life, we know that everything that happens can help us to achieve it or deflect us from it: as we study the things He made, we can develop in love of God by loving all that He loves, our fellow men above all. But there is the steady drag downward too, the drag away from God towards more immediate satisfactions, with every yielding to the drag diminishing us as men. When we fail, we know what we are doing, and there is a certain gloomy luxury even in that. When the effort to keep moving towards the goal costs us even agonizingly, we know what gain to set against the agony.

3

How are we so to handle ourselves and our lives that we may grow towards our goal? That is what the Moral Law, clarified and developed by Christ as we have seen, especially in Chapter VII on his Values and Priorities, is there to tell us. Our tendency is to think of the Moral Law as a set of prohibitions blocking off all sorts of fascinating possibilities: stunting our personalities with its bleak negatives—with ourselves rather noble for obeying them, and hoping that heaven will be an adequate reward for all we are giving up by not sinning.

But this is baby talk. We would not dream of talking like that about the instructions Ford or Morris gives for the right running of a car. The laws of morality are Maker's instructions for the right running of ourselves.

We do not grumble at the maker of the car for limiting our freedom to use it as we like, we thank him for telling us. No sane man would knowingly use the car as its maker says he should not. Apply these tests to ourselves and our Maker, then begin wondering just how sane we are. Do we thank God for all those "Thou shalt nots" as we should thank Ford or Morris? And God knows how often we decide to use ourselves as God says we should not.

Virtue, I need hardly say, is not simply the absence of sin: there is no virtue in refusing to commit the sins we have no taste for anyhow. Virtue is the right direction of energy, and the laws of morality tell us what the right direction is: they are all ways of applying the law of love to our relations with God and men. Lacking their guidance, men can only follow inclination. Spiritually they get flabbier and flabbier. For the soul's muscles, like the body's, grow by effort, and there is no effort in following the line of least resistance. So they are not happy, feel all-overish, wonder if life is worthwhile, suffer in fact from a kind of spiritual liverishness. The effort that would tone them up spiritually they see no reason to make, not even suspecting that the laws of morality are Maker's instructions.

All energy, all health therefore, is in living rightly. The notion that the sinner is vital and the saint a languid, pallid person is strongly entrenched. The truth is exactly the opposite. To quote Chesterton,

If you think virtue is languor,
Just try it and see.

Even one who does not accept Christ's teaching on Trinity and Incarnation, on re-birth and Eternal life, can see a superb practicality in his rules for life here on earth. One sees no competing view of what life is about which could have any such possibility of success, and to hope for an integrated world order or national order without one is sub-Utopian.

Yet, to repeat, in order to be effective Christ's redeeming power has to be applied, to the individual and to society. Whenever it has been applied to the individual, it has proved its power, splendidly often enough, but to some extent in all—no Christian does not know that however mediocre he may in fact be, he would have been far worse without it. For effectiveness it has to be applied to the social order too, and this is more difficult because it involves its acceptance by millions who do not accept him. What kind of agreement upon Christ's principles for human life is to be expected of a world in which two thousand million people know nothing of Christ, and dislike what they know of Christians?

To produce that general acceptance of his way of life for mankind at large looks like being a slow business. It might be hastened by agreement among those who have accepted him, it would be really speeded up if our acceptance showed more in our lives.

It is God's way to will into existence not the completeness of anything but that which, in His providence, will grow to completeness. The act of creation, for instance, was a beginning of creation, the material universe started on a road which has brought our world to the condition in which it now is, on which it will certainly continue, and continue to develop—"There will be a new heaven and a new earth *in which righteousness dwells"* (2 Peter 3.13). The last four words remind us that the kingdom of righteousness too, like the universe in which it is and the beings of whom it is made, is growing towards what it is to be.

4

The kingdom of God is here, growing (with painful slowness, we may feel) towards its fullness: the Mystical Body of Christ is a reality. The citizens of the kingdom, the cells of the Body, says Jesus, are to be the leaven that leavens the whole lump of mankind. But until the leavening is complete, one is aware only of the lump. And it is not only the mass of humanity that needs leavening, but each Christian.

No one metaphor will cover all the complexities. We are in the kingdom: we are on the road—the road that is meant to lead each man all the way from God who created him to God with whom he is to attain full union. The rules of life on the road we have been considering. Of themselves these would revolutionize the world—if only we would let them revolutionize us. But as we have seen, we live two lives—the natural life which we have by being born into the human race, the supernatural life of grace which we have by being re-born into Christ. In the harmonizing of these two lives lies our integrity: and the effort is lifelong. We may or may not think that men have a tendency to evil, but at least we have a tendency to go after what we want, and there's plenty of evil towards which we have plenty of tendency.

As it is, we are a continuing problem to those who

have no religious beliefs of their own. The most persistent reaction runs in some such terms as these: "If I believed what Christians say they believe, I wouldn't sin —I wouldn't dare to, and I wouldn't want to. But Christians do sin, very much like other people. So they don't really believe."

There is an even tougher objection—how is it possible for a man, reborn into Christ, who has all the powers sanctifying grace gives, to act as if he hadn't? That is not one of the questions people ask us, because they haven't a notion of re-birth or of what sanctifying grace means to us; it is one we ask ourselves, desperately. Anyhow, the first objection is tough enough. My own guess is that it is the principal reason why people don't join the Church. In the practical order, the strongest argument against the Faith is ourselves! For our own sake, quite apart from the objector's, we should take a good look at it. Why, believing as we do, do we behave as we do?

Part of the answer is that it is quite possible to believe, and sincerely believe, that the Church teaches truths entrusted to her by God, and yet never bother to learn what these truths are and what flows from them, holding them only as formulas, strings of words—their illuminating power, their vitalizing power, unused. This sort of unconcern can issue in sheer stupidity— people asking, How much can I have of the pleasures of this world without losing heaven? They are rather like a child at the party wondering just how much he can eat without being sick on the carpet: he usually *is* sick on the carpet.

Short of that foolish limit, it is possible for people who would die for Christ to give very little thought to what God is saying through him. In living their daily lives, they conform easily enough to what is customary in their social group: what everybody does can't be so very wrong. If they are ordered to face a particular moral issue, they cannot believe that God actually demands as much as that, they themselves wouldn't if they were God. Yet when the chips are really down, people in this state would die rather than deny Christ, and willingness to die is a sure test of belief. Even a failure of courage at the crisis moment would not mean that the belief was not genuine, as Peter knew: the shame at failure could be its own kind of evidence of the genuineness of the belief.

But even those who know, even know very profoundly, what the doctrines mean, can sin. The outsider looking in at us would expect that the immensities we believe would revolutionize our lives, make us new men. We know better. It may puzzle us, but it is quite undeniable that, illuminated by such truths, nourished by such sacraments, we are so horribly like everybody else. There are moments when we feel as if we were two people, one believing firmly, the other acting dead against what we believe. If we are serious, we have to try to find out why. One way or another, the answer lies in the distinction between knowing and realizing.

The world about us seems so much more real than God. We know it is not, of course, but that's how we *feel*. The world presses in on us through all five senses (plus some ways more intimate); it solicits us through every appetite. God does none of these things. Spiritual reality cannot be seen, tasted, smelt, felt, it has no access to the imagination, it makes no pictures. The sheer intensity of the here-and-now pleasure that sin promises is not matched by anything religion counter-offers. The allure of sin so often seems irresistible, the allure of virtue so very resistible. We may decide to grab the immediate pleasure and damn the consequences—which is a fair statement of what sin is. But at least we know what consequences we are damning. We have left the right road, but we know where the road is and how to get back onto it.

Yet, to return to the objection we are considering, the *belief* is as real as the pressure from sin. The conflict is no sham fight. Grace aiding, Christ aiding, faith can win. In this life the victory is never certain, and often looks hopeless. Yet two things must not be forgotten. (1) The man who believes with full understanding cannot help feeling a fool even in the high moment of sin, for he knows what he is imperilling, and that takes some of the glow out of sin's victories.

(2) And it is a fact of experience that a man may sin spectacularly yet suffer death rather than deny Christ. The acid test of belief is the willingness to die for it. The acid test of realization is ability to live by it.

The feeling that Christ is something special is pretty universal in our world. But there is not much actual detail in it. Even Christians seem content to know very little about him. Take a quick example of knowledge that ought to be there but is not always. Once only in the Gospels we are told that he was joyful (Luke 15.21). If we were really interested in him, that solitary occasion would surely stand out like a star. But you would be surprised at the number of Christians who do not know what he was joyful about. There is a combination of reverence and vagueness, there is even today a combination of enthusiasm for him and vagueness about him, in which it is not possible to know what I have called his practicality, the score of ways in which he actually matters to us here and now. The luxury of knowing what life is all about, what we are, why we are here, where we are supposed to be going, is all grounded in him. He gave it to us, but we must know what he actually gave.

Further, he has taught us how—reality being as he has shown it—we should act. And the key to action he has given us is love. We are to love God with every element in us; we are to love our fellow men with the same kind of love we have for ourselves. And this without any limit at all: we are to love our enemies, do good to them that hate us. And the supreme proof of love is willingness to lay down our life.

He not only taught it, but as a last fine edge of practicality he did it, did all of it. He laid down his life, he loved his enemies, he did good to them that hated him. Nailed to the Cross, he prayed for his slayers: "Father, forgive them, for they know not what they do." He had told us that he who loses his life shall save it: this we might have taken as pious rhetoric, not meant to be followed out to the letter. But he lost his life, and he saved it. Death took him, but could not hold him. It will take us, but will not hold us either. He conquered death for us, not for himself only.

My verbs so far have been in the past tense: he taught, he loved, he did good, death took him, death could not hold him. But his value for us lies not only in what he did but in what he is now doing. He did not only set us an example, and leave us to follow. He did not only give us a set of truths about God and life and ourselves, and leave us to live by them. He himself is living in us *now,* if we will let him.

Index